TEACHING PEOPLE
TO LOVE THEMSELVES

D0877713

Second Revised Edition

by
DOV PERETZ ELKINS, M.H.L., D. Min.

A Leader's Handbook of Theory and Technique
for Self-Esteem and Affirmation Training

Preface by Dr. Jack Canfield

GROWTH ASSOCIATES
Human Relations Consultants and Publishers
22 Governors Lane
Princeton, NJ 08540-3668
Toll Free: 1-866-368-8672
Office@JewishGrowth.org
www.JewishGrowth.org

Copyright © 1977, 1978—Dov Peretz Elkins
ISBN: 0-918834-06-6
Library of Congress Catalog Card Number 78-61670
Printed in the United States of America
All Rights Reserved
Cover Design by Marcia Smith
Fourth Printing, 2010

Growth Associates
Human Relations Consultants and Publishers
22 Governors Lane
Princeton, NJ 08540-3668
Toll Free: 1-866-368-8672
Office@JewishGrowth.org
www.JewishGrowth.org

Also available from Growth Associates:
Glad To Be Me: Building Self-Esteem in Yourself and Others
Edited by Dr. Dov Peretz Elkins
Self Concept Sourcebook, Edited by Dr. Dov Peretz Elkins
Twelve Pathways to Feeling Better About Yourself by Dov Peretz Elkins
Please send for order blank.
For information about training workshops and consultation in the area of self-concept, human relations training, humanistic education, and organization development, led by Dr. Elkins, write or call Growth Associates.

Dr. Dov. Peretz Elkins is author and editor of fifteen books on theology, psychology and education. He is known throughout the United States and Canada for his work as lecturer, human relations consultant and trainer, counselor, author, educator, rabbi, and organization development specialist.

*****

Thanks are expressed to my teachers, Professors Edward Thornton, James B. Ashbrook, Gayraud Wilmore, and Mr. Paul McVey, for their guidance in writing this book. Responsibility for its weaknesses lies with the author alone. Special appreciation goes to Sidney B. Simon, Howard Kirschenbaum, Jack Canfield and Carl Struever for helping me understand the importance of self-esteem. Finally, the author is grateful to Pearl Ostroff for her help in preparing the manuscript and for tolerating an often impatient author.

**DEDICATED TO
JACK CANFIELD
—BROTHER IN SPIRIT—**

TABLE OF CONTENTS

PREFACE

I have known Dov for the last four years and have co-led several workshops on self-concept development with him. Dov is a person who loves life and seeks to evoke, validate and affirm the life force within each person he works with. It is a delight to now have this book which manifests those same positive qualities through the printed media. Each exercise in this valuable sourcebook—supported by cogent rationale and theory—seeks to enhance the essential joy of being that is our birthright but which has been lost to so many of us through our experiences of negatively focused parenting, our negatively focused educational system and the pervasive alienation of our culture in general.

Dov provides us with numerous methods to help ourselves and the people we work with develop a positive self regard, a strong personal power base from which to operate more effectively in the world. Each of us seeks desperately to be validated by our fellow human beings, to be told that we are OK, loveable and worthy of attention. We each seek the fulfillment of our basic needs of warmth, comfort, contact and communication...and yet our society has not taught us how to attain these strokes nor how to give them to others. Indeed, we have been taught to be cautious, self-controlled, self-effacing and self destructive.

Here in one volume is a priceless collection of activities and techniques which help people learn to love themselves and each other in a group context of trust, openness and validation. The self-esteem groups described in this book and which Dov and I have led in numerous settings create an atmosphere of acceptance, love, encouragement and support. Each group becomes a kind of "second chance family" in which each participant has the opportunity to receive the validation, support and permission to be and to do that may have been insufficient or lacking altogether in their family of origin.

Dov has provided an easy-to-read and inspiring introduction which outlines the function of self-esteem and the need for its development in both schools and in counselling groups. He has drawn his ideas from a variety of personal growth theories and disciplines and his synthesis is uniquely useful. Even though we had worked together often, I found several new and important points to consider.

The most valuable aspect of this handbook, however, is its collection of activities, techniques and group methods which enhance self-esteem. And they do work. I have seen them used over and over in group after group with astounding success. While many of these techniques are likely to be familiar to the experienced group leader, it is extremely valuable to find them all together in one sourcebook. To help the less experienced leader Dov has also provided two different designs for short and long-term workshops. These designs are the result of much experience in the field and are a useful resource.

Finally...a note of caution to those of you who may be doing this work for the first time. Anyone can buy a book of activities—there are numerous ones available these days—and guide a group of people through the various steps of an exercise. This is a relatively easy thing to do. But you must be aware that many of these exercises—while seemingly simple enough when you read them—can evoke strong emotional reactions in people. For every drive toward wholeness there is an equally powerful impulse toward resistance—the result of years of negative programming, hurt and pain. As one begins to recover his or her selfhood, one may re-experience the internalized negativity and fear that this has created. This is not to be taken lightly or the exercises will take on a superficial quality—an unreal over-simplification of the process of growth. It must be understood that it is OK to experience one's sadness, one's happiness, one's anger and one's helplessness as well as one's strengths, one's happiness, one's power and one's ecstasy. It is therefore crucial that you make every effort to first experience these activities yourself and be aware of their potential.

Helping people to become who they really are and who they are capable of becoming is very sacred work. It is a form of psychological and spiritual midwifery. It is in every sense of the word a process of rebirth—of being reborn to our essential nature. There are many teachers and many methods. Enhancing self-esteem is one of the most important paths. We are all fortunate that Dov has given us this very valuable fruit of his labors.

Jack Canfield
Director
Institute for Wholistic Education

Chapter 1

THEORETICAL BACKGROUND

The concept of self-esteem has been the subject of intense investigation on the part of psychologists and theologians for decades. [1] To those subscribing to the viewpoints of humanistic psychology, such as Rogers, Fitts, Maslow, Bugental, and Otto, [2] the self and how one sees oneself are more important determinants of healthy personality and personal effectiveness than the sex drive, repressed memories of early childhood and environmental stimuli, as the other major schools of psychoanalysis and behaviorism have assumed. The unique and personal meanings which a person's experience has for himself is the only reality he knows. His own phenomenal field, of which the self is a major part, is the crucial variable in determining how a person will react to the world.

Humanistic psychology focuses on growth and self-actualization rather than psychopathology. [3] The fulfillment of one's latent potential, the achievement of a fully-functioning, socially effective personality, is its goal. [4] In striving to achieve the goal of a self-actualizing way of life, one's self-concept plays a highly significant role. [5]

If a person sees himself as a worthwhile, useful, lovable, competent human being, he will be able to lead a happy and productive life. If, on the other hand, he feels himself to be worthless, unlovable and incompetent, his life will be plagued with self-doubt, self-pity, interpersonal ineffectiveness, and lack of success in all that he does. [6]

Maslow sees self-esteem as a basic need of the personality. Just as the body requires calcium and other vitamins to be healthy, so the personality, in the same biological, organismic way, needs esteem from others and from self to achieve emotional health and self-actualization. [7]

Maslow posits three major antecedents of high self-esteem: [8] "respect and approval from other people;" "actual capacity, achievement, and success;" and "acceptance of and acting upon our own inner nature."

It will not be within the purview of the self-esteem laboratory deal with or measure achievement or success in life. What will be provided are opportunities to provide and receive respect and approval to and from others. In our view this leads to greater acceptance of self and the increased ability to act upon one's own inner nature. With a renewed sense of respect and approval from others and self, and an increased ability to be more self-accepting, we assume new successes and achievements in the outside world will follow.

ASSUMPTIONS

Three essential theoretical components combine to create the writer's approach to self-esteem group training. These include my training in Jewish theology and in humanistic psychology, and my training and experience in laboratory education.

I shall delineate the basic assumptions that I bring to the work of self-esteem group training from these three areas.

Jewish Theology

Two major strands in Jewish theology and ethics impinge upon the subject of a person's self concept. First is the Jewish attitude of sanctity and uniqueness of each human creature. Second is a corollary to this viewpoint, namely, that since humans are made in the divine image, they must be treated with respect and affirmation by their fellow human beings.

The Bible describes persons as created in the image of God,[9] a lofty and noble formulation clothing human beings in dignity and significance. Besides being made in the divine image, man is made "but little lower than the angels."[10] Furthermore, all persons are united in their common humanity through being the creatures of one God. "Have we not all one Father? Has not one God created us?"[11]

Since persons were created in the divine image, they are seen as sharing in the essence of God's holiness. "You shall be holy, for I the Lord your God am holy."[12] The late Rabbi Abraham Joshua Heschel warned that "the future of the human species depends upon our degree of reverence for the individual man."[13] In a related statement, Heschel avers: "The degree to which one is sensitive to other people's suffering, to other men's humanity, is the index of one's own humanity."[14]

The Mishnah, the rabbinic collection of ancient Hebrew law edited in the year 200 C. E., sums up the implications of the biblical view of personhood in terms of the uniqueness, significance and the infinite worth of human life:[15]

Why was only a single man created? To teach that for him who destroys one life, it is regarded as though he had destroyed all men, and that for him who saves one life, it is regarded as though he had saved the whole world. Furthermore, it was for the sake of peace, so that man might not say to his fellowman, "My father was greater than your father." Another reason is to proclaim that greatness of the Holy One. For man stamps many coins with one seal and they are all alike; but the King of Kings has stamped every man with the seal of the first man, yet not one of them is like his fellow. Therefore everyone must say: For my sake was the world created.

Humans in the Hebrew view are thus sacred creatures of God, made in His own image, with unique qualities and attributes of their own which are to be actualized during their brief journey on earth. An obvious implication of this extraordinary view of persons is that they must treat themselves with great care, pride and dignity. How arrogant it sounds to say that "For my sake the world was created." Yet it is this "arrogance" and self-affirmation which Judaism demands.

Not only must persons treat themselves nobly, but they must also treat others in the same way. "He who oppresses the poor blasphemes his Maker. He who is gracious to the needy honors Him."[16] The way we treat each other is a reflection upon our belief in God our Creator. Any diminution of a person's dignity is an insult to the Creator.

This biblical and talmudic attitude of the dignity, uniqueness and sanctity of human beings is the setting for the Jewish view that one must love oneself and care for oneself. This is not to be a conditional self-love. It does not mean that one should love oneself if he has a high intelligence, or an unusual artistic talent, or if he has achieved great things in life. Persons should love themselves because they are made in the divine image, because they are creatures of God, and because God made them to be unique and worthy persons.

Jewish tradition states clearly that self-love is an important attitude for one to hold, and a prerequisite for ethical behavior.

"Love your neighbor as yourself,"[17] implies that in order to love one's neighbor one must love oneself. In other words, love your neighbor as much as you love yourself. The Torah need not command us to love ourselves, it is assumed that we will, that we do.

In the Mishnaic tractate **Ethics of the Fathers,** Rabbi Eliezer states: "Let your friend's honor be as important to you as your own."[18] Again, honoring oneself is assumed. That self-honor then becomes a model of how we should honor others, just as self-love, in the biblical verse above, is a model for the love of others.

In another passage in **Ethics of the Fathers,** Rabbi Simeon states in one of the clearest formulations of the command to think highly of oneself anywhere in rabbinic literature, "Be not wicked in your own esteem."[19] The negative formulation is probably a reflection of Rabbi Simeon's observation that most people **do** hold themselves in low esteem and need to be reminded not to do so. His admonition is a more psychologically acceptable way to say: Hold yourself in high esteem.

The ancient sage Hillel's statement on self-care and self-affirmation is perhaps the most widely quoted rabbinic saying on the subject. "If I am not for myself, who will be?"[20] It is one's duty to be his own guardian. It is a fact of life that if a person does not care for himself, nourish himself, be his own advocate, he cannot expect others to care for him.

And yet the second part of Hillel's saying gives balance and perspective to the need for self-concern. "If I am for myself alone, what am I?'[21]

This introduces the subject of self versus others. Is not too much self-love destructive toward a world view that is emotionally healthy and ethically sound? Theologians have argued thus for many centuries. Bernard Loomer, former Professor of Theology at The Divinity School, University of Chicago, says about Reinhold Niebuhr's view that too much self-love is man's downfall:[22]

> . . . .we can say that for Niebuhr (and for much if not most of the history of Christian theology) man sins or contributes to his own downfall because he is strong and not because he is weak. His trouble stems from excess and not deficiency. Basically, man tends to think more rather than less highly of himself than he ought to think.

My view is that the excess of pride and strength that are destructive to man are the veneer that hide low self-esteem and lack of self-love. Self-love and self-respect are minimal requisites for a healthy personality and for a fully functioning person. But proper self-love is not complete unless it leads also to love of others. Full and authentic self-love will spill over to others, whereas the absence of self-love will prevent a person from loving others. It is for this reason that Hillel can say that "If I am not for myself, who will be?" and complete his question with the natural corollary to self-love, namely, "If I am for myself alone, what am I?"[21]

Maslow discusses self-esteem similarly when he says that "To invent or create you must have the 'arrogance of creativeness' which so many investigators have noticed. But, of course, if you have **only** the arrogance without the humility, then you are in fact paranoid. You **must** be aware not only of the godlike possibilities within, but also of the existential human limitations. You must be able simultaneously to laugh at yourself and at all human pretensions."[23]

It is this very same balance between pride and humility, self-love and love for others, creativity and existential human limitations, that is alluded to in the popular Hasidic aphorism of Rabbi Bunam, who said that each person should carry two pieces of paper in his pockets. On one it should say, "For my sake the world was created."[24] In the other pocket it should say, "I am but dust and ashes."[25]

What Rabbi Bunam is saying is that there must exist within man a carefully balanced tension between self-confidence and humility, between the person's recognition of being made in the divine image, and yet at the same time knowing that one is in fact not God. The parallel attitude in humanistic psychology to this Jewish viewpoint would be that high self-esteem is created only when one accepts his weaknesses and foibles and limitations. Sinful pride and selfish arrogance go along with not seeing oneself as mortal, but as sovereign and totally independent of others. One must make a careful distinction between selfishness and high self-esteem. The former results from low self-esteem and is an attempt to cover up or compensate for self-hate. One who does not love himself is so preoccupied with his own needs that he does not see or care for others, and thus manifests selfishness. He who truly loves himself will be free from narcissism and hence be able to share himself, his life, his love, with and for others. The illness of narcissism is the result of low self-esteem, not the overabundance of it. As Erich Fromm put it, "Selfishness and self-love, far from being identical, are actually opposites. The selfish person does not love himself too much but too little; in fact he hates himself. . . ."[26]

Coexisting with the ancient rabbinic admonitions for self-love are frequent warnings to remain humble and pious. Again, these are not contradictory but complementary. For example, Rabbi Levitas of Yavneh said: "Be exceedingly lowly of spirit for the expectation of mortal man is that he will turn to worms."[27] Rabbi Jannai warned, "Be a tail to lions and not a head to foxes."[28] Hillel, eloquent advocate of self-care, is the author of many talmudic statements recommending humility as the path for man to follow. "A name that is too widely publicized is a name that is lost."[29]

Humility and self-love are counterparts because the highest form of self-affirmation grows out of deep faith in the Creator of life. He who is Ultimate Good has created a good world and good creatures to inhabit it.

Being humble enough to accept the Creator and trust in him, one can allow the affirmation of the Creator to spill over to his own self-affirmation. Claudio Naranjo explains that "In religious terms, this process can be described as one in which man rediscovers his cosubstantiality with the divine nature, and comes closer to seeing the world and himself as God did on the seventh day of Genesis, when He saw that His creation was good."[30] In similar vein, Paul Tillich writes that Spinoza derived the idea of self-affirmation of man "from the self-affirmation of the divine substance in which he participates. In a similar way all mystics draw their power of self-affirmation from the experience of the power of being-itself with which they are united."[31]

Thus, one can affirm himself and love himself ultimately because he is a creature of a beneficent Creator. The person is good because God made him good, unconditionally. If one accepts his being made in the divine image, with all the beauty, marvel and mystery that this implies, as well as the finitude and mortality of being a creature, then his self-esteem can be authentically high.

Harry Stack Sullivan stressed the importance of "reflected appraisals" in creating one's self-image. As a child matures, he is flooded with an endless stream of interpersonal relationships which bring positive or negative attitudes toward himself as he assimilates the views of significant others.[32] In similar fashion, Judaism has always stressed the importance of sound interpersonal relationships in fostering personal happiness and ethical living. The community is the crucible in which a well-rounded person is created. It is human encounter, the existential meeting of two persons in meaningful relationship, which is the spark that ignites the enormous potential of human energy and creativity. What Buber later described as an I-Thou relationship was foreseen and stated by Choni Ha-meagel two thousand years ago in the Talmud: "Community or death."[33]

Whether it be in the family, the neighborhood, the synagogue, or other institutions, persons learn and grow through interpersonal relationships. Hillel, whose wisdom we have cited earlier, said that one must not separate himself from the community.[34] Jews cannot recite their most sacred prayers without a quorum of ten adults. Weddings, funerals, circumcision ceremonies, and other significant personal and community occasions must be sanctified by the presence of the **minyan,** the holy community. "All Israel is one family." "All Israel is responsible for one another." Such statements of the need for community have been the hallmark of Jewish survival for four thousand years. Gentiles continue to marvel at the closeness of the family, the sense of community, which exists among Jews and Jewish communities throughout the world.

In Elie Wiesel's book on Hasidism, **Souls on Fire,**[35] we see a Hasidic view of fulfilling our highest spiritual nature and realizing our deepest inner potential through human relatedness:

Every encounter quickens the steps of the Redeemer; let two things become one and the world is no longer the same; let two human creatures accept one another and creation will have meaning, the meaning they will have imposed upon it.

The Jewish dream of a messianic age, as described by Isaiah (chapters 2 and 11, for example), of universal peace and harmony among humans and animals, is a vision not unlike the humanized societies pictured by Charles Reich, [36] or the age of synergizing and actualizing human beings described by Maslow in his descriptions of "Eupsychia." [37]

An essential quality of the new humanizing society will be the affirmation of persons by their fellow humans. The ideal Jewish community is one in which the "reflected appraisals" of each person for his fellow are given out of love. Such appraisals will be essentially affirmations, whether they be praise or criticism. Humans will affirm their neighbor as a fellow member of humanity.

Rabbinic literature abounds in warnings not to lower man's own estimation of himself through disvalidation, slander, and gossip. The disciples of Rabbi Nechuniah asked him, "Why have you merited long life?" His reply was that "I have never tried to elevate myself at the expense of my neighbors." [38] Another talmudic sage predicted that "All who go down to Gehennum (Hell) will arise, except for one who shames his neighbor publicly and he who calls his neighbor by a derogatory name." [39] In the rabbinic view, the devaluation of one's self-image was worse than bodily harm. [40] When Hillel found a poor man who was formerly wealthy, he not only gave him charity, but also a horse to help him farm, and a slave to attend upon him. [41] Thus, charity was dispensed not only according to one's physical needs, but also according to one's psychological needs, in consonance with one's self image. Affirmation of one's fellow person included more than merely a monetary handout. It included concern for one's sense of self-respect.

Slander, a vicious form of disvalidation, is among the most heinous of sins in the Jewish ethical system. It is more destructive than murder, for one who commits murder kills only one individual, while a person who slanders his fellow destroys three lives: himself for uttering it, his listener, and the one about whom it is said. [42] Eleven of the forty-four sins catalogued in the Yom Kippur Confessional (**Al Chet**) deal with sins of the tongue, for one's propensity to slander his neighbor is great, and the effects of such disvalidation are enormously destructive. Slandering one's fellow is more than even the psychological destruction of another human being. It denies the essence of God, the Source of all life and the essence of being-itself. "Whoever utters slander is denying the very essence of his faith." [43]

The new age of the humanized, eupsychian society will be one in which children will grow in an atmosphere of trust, love, and affirmation. It will be the age of the Messiah, when inner harmony and international peace and fulfillment will reign throughout the world. This new age of self-actualizing humanity will be marked by a healthy sense of self-trust and self-acceptance in each individual, followed by self-respect and self-love. These are the building blocks upon which Eupsychia, the Messianic Era, must ultimately rise.

...the Maggid wished his disciplines to develop confidence in their own powers; failing that, they could not adequately discharge themselves of their rabbinical functions. Flagrant display of pride? Perhaps. But since man and especially Just Man is created in God's image, he may and must, under certain circumstances, assume one or another of His attributes.... "God's cloak is humility," was interpreted in Mezeritch as meaning: humility should be like a cloak; one must know how to take it off sometimes. [44]

Humanistic Psychology

The second set of assumptions which undergird self-esteem group train- is rooted in humanistic psychology. This so-called "third force" stresses the human qualities of persons. It sees human beings as valuing creatures who combine physical, rational, emotional and spiritual components into holistic and integrated beings in the process of becoming.

Humanistic psychology assumes that one's existential and subjective view of self is more determinative of who one is than both one's physical environment and childhood experiences. One's own phenomenal world, including the possibilities and limits one envisages for his life, his goals, his ideals, his openness to experience and his ability to be consciously aware of his experience, is more important for his behavior than most of the objective factors that circumscribe his existence. If one views one's core personality as basically good, useful, competent, lovable, and satisfied, one's life will be constructive, useful, meaningful, and productive. If not, one will suffer from anxiety, unhappiness, a failure to fulfill one's potential, and a wasting away of one's energy and creativity.

For this reason self-esteem is a fundamental psychological model for understanding human beings. It is a phenomenological model, leaving much to one's own conscious awareness of oneself. It is a model which can include all of the values and beauty of life as I see them from my experiential and intellectual viewpoints. It enables me to encompass the kinds of intangible values which I consider to be more important to human life than all the definable and measurable aspects of human existence.

A. J. Sutich sees humanistic psychology as scientifically based, yet going beyond science. It is "an orientation toward the whole of psychology rather than a distinct area or school. It stands for respect for the worth of persons, respect for differences of approach, openmindedness as to acceptable methods, and interest in exploration of new aspects of human behavior.... It is concerned with topics having little place in existing theories and systems: e.g., love, creativity, self, growth, organism, basic need gratification, self-actualization, higher values, being, becoming, spontaneity, play, humor, affection, naturalness, warmth, ego-transcendence, objectivity, autonomy, responsibility, meaning, fair-play, transcendental experience, peak experience, courage, and related concepts." [45]

Since humanistic psychology emphasizes the person's own present consciousness, rather than his environment or psychological history, the notion of self-esteem looms large within it. If one's view of self and world determine one's feelings and behavior, then a positive self-concept is a crucial determinant for personality health and full humanness.

Carl Rogers and his students have developed a scheme of the fully-functioning person generally referred to as "self theory." Rogers summarizes this theory in the outline below: [46]

A. The individual has an inherent tendency toward **actualizing** his organism.

B. The individual has the capacity and tendency to **symbolize experiences** accurately in **awareness**. [47]

1. A corollary statement is that he has the capacity and tendency to keep his **self-concept** congruent with his **experience**.

C. The individual has a **need for positive regard.**

D. The individual has a **need for positive self-regard.**

E. Tendencies A and B are most fully realized when needs C and D are met. More specifically, tendencies A and B tend to be most fully realized when

1. The individual **experiences unconditional positive regard** from significant others.

2. The pervasiveness of this **unconditional positive regard** is made evident through relationships marked by a complete and communicated **empathic** understanding of the individual's **frame of reference.**

F. If the conditions under E are met to a maximum degree, the individual who experiences these conditions will be a fully functioning person.

Based on "self theory" more recent studies suggest that self-esteem is a suitably definitive concept by which to explain variances in the level of effective behavior, and that it can provide the basis for a new theoretical model of personality functioning. [48] Maslow, for example, suggests that finding out what a person is really like "inside, deep down," is the key to creating a successful personality. [49] High self-esteem is a prerequisite for trusting one's organism sufficiently to rely upon it as the locus of evaluation, and to search out one's true nature for the purpose of using it as ultimate guide in life. Only persons who like and respect themselves are able to realize their full potential. A fully human person is one who trusts himself enough to carry forward his deepest inner hopes and most daring visions through which he strives to reach his highest potential.

I would summarize my beliefs about the nature of personhood deriving from principles of Jewish theology and humanistic psychology, as well as from personal growth experiences at such places as National Training Laboratories and Esalen Institute, and including my own personal psychotherapy, as follows:

1) the person is by basic nature clothed in dignity, meaning and value

2) the person has a natural tendency toward growth, health and self-actualization [50]

3) the nature of human beings includes more than their intellect, body and feelings, but also a dimension which is spiritual in nature

4) human relationships are the crucible for forming and fulfilling a health personality

5) each person is unique as well as possessing species-wide directional tendencies

6) all persons fulfill only a small fraction of their potential and can learn new ways of reaching more and more of that potential [51]

7) when one's subjective view of oneself is congruent with one's experience, one can reach toward full human evolution

8) a person with high self-esteem will be best able to achieve the qualities of personality health: increasing openness to experience, **increasing existential living, and increasing trust in one's organism.** [52]

Laboratory Education

The third set of assumptions which are the basis of self-esteem group training grow out of my experience as a participant in and facilitator of laboratory learning.

A new model of learning has grown up in America over the past twenty-five years, often called sensitivity training, and now better known as laboratory learning. Laboratory learning is a group experience that provides participants with opportunities to learn more about themselves, their feelings and behaviors. It involves interpersonal experiences which can be analyzed in terms of generalizations and applications for "back-home" living. The optimum atmosphere in laboratory learning is one of mutual trust and authenticity in which learners can behave with a minimum of defensiveness. Laboratory learning combines experiential learning and conceptualization, often involving development of new interpersonal skills through the examination of one's values, attitudes and behaviors, and their effects upon self and others.

Several assumptions of laboratory education undergird the self-esteem lab. The first of these is that the most important subject of learning is the self.

Clark · E. Moustakas enumerates several principles which connect effective learning and self-concept: [53]

• Behavior can best be understood from the individual's own point of view

• The individual responds in such ways as to be consistent with himself

• The individual's perception of himself determines how he will behave

• As long as the individual accepts himself, he will continue to grow and develop his potentialities. When he does not accept himself, much of his energies will be used to defend rather than explore and to actualize himself.

• An individual learns significantly only those things which are involved in the maintenance or enhancement of self.

In an experiment performed over a quarter of a century ago, James

Benjamins asked forty-eight high school students to rank their performances on an intelligence test. The students were then given false reports one level below or above their predictions. Given the test a second time, they performed in the direction of the falsely reported results. Those who thought they had done better than expected improved on the second chance. Those told that they did worse than they expected actually did so in the second test.[54] Countless studies show how self-perception is crucial in learning and growth.[55]

A second assumption concerning laboratory education is that the learner grows most when he accepts responsibility for his own learning, including his goals and their implementation. George Brown, in applying Gestalt Therapy to the classroom, states that effective learning must proceed from "subject matter which is closely related to the significant personal needs and feelings of the students. The major criterion for inclusion of any subject is the extent to which (students) can come to feel significantly related to it."[56]

Carl Rogers makes the same observation when he points out that **"anything that can be taught to another is relatively inconsequential, and has little or no significant influence on behavior."**[57]

A third assumption about effective learning in a laboratory setting is that the most long-lasting learnings are those which affect a person as a whole, including mind, emotions, body awareness, imagination and spirituality. As William Schutz pointed out, "man is a unified being and functions on many levels at once: physical, emotional, intellectual, interpersonal, social, and spiritual. These levels are intimately interrelated, and actions on any one level are inevitably accompanied by actions on all others."[58]

Terms such as "affective education" or "confluent education" are becoming popular. They stress the emotional, or feeling component, of the educational process, as well as the cognitive. In a setting of laboratory education, where personal growth is the goal, feelings are recognized and dealt with openly. Only through greater awareness of one's feelings can the learner choose to express, or postpone expression of, the feelings which well up within. To deny or repress them prevents learning. An open and safe climate in which the learner can risk admitting and expressing deep emotions is the most congenial atmosphere in which human growth takes place.

A fourth assumption is that learning implies changing attitudes, values and behaviors, and not merely rote memorization of facts and information. Accepting a new viewpoint about life, about self, about the world, or a new way of acting and relating, are the most significant ways in which a person can change. Alfred H. Gorman defines learning simply as "a change in behavior."[59]

The fifth and last assumption about laboratory learning is the most crucial of all, that the best learning is based on **experience.** Modern methodologies of experience-based learning are derived largely from the pioneering work of John Dewey whose viewpoint was that people learn after reflecting upon and evaluating their life experience.[60] The school and the classroom are artificial devices for helping children learn. Insofar as the classroom is a microcosm of the outside world it can succeed in constituting a wholesome environment in which significant learning may take place. But most classrooms are places for lecturing and reading and testing rather than experiencing.

Laboratory education succeeds insofar as it simulates life outside. The difference will be in the safety and openness of the laboratory atmosphere. The facilitator may introduce a structured experience, which is then followed by discussing and evaluating the experience to see what learnings might derive from it and how these learnings can be applied to life.

John E. Jones and J. William Pfeiffer, directors of University Associates, a consulting and publishing firm which trains human relations trainers, have published a series of Annual Handbooks on the theory and practice of experience-based learning, including collections of structured experiences. [61] They conceptualize a continuum of learning from the least experiential to the most experiential in ten stages. These are, in order of increasingly experiential learning:

> reading
> lecture
> experiential lecture
> discussion
> participation training
> case study
> role playing
> instrumentation
> structured experience
> intensive growth group

The self-esteem laboratory is designed mainly around the ninth level of learning: structured experience. It is the contention of the University Associates leadership that in the more experiential approaches, stressing active participant involvement instead of passive receptivity, "the learning is presumably internalized more effectively." [62]

Jones and Pfeiffer present a model of how to use the structured experience, which goes through five steps, [63] including **experiencing;** sharing—or, **publishing**—reactions; **processing**—evaluating the experience; **generalizing,** or the development of principles extracted from the experience; and **applying** new learnings to life.

These assumptions about learning and growth, together with the theological and psychological assumptions about personhood described above, constitute the theoretical basis of the self-esteem laboratory.

FOOTNOTES

1. See, for example, Carl Rogers, **Client-Centered Therapy**, (Boston: Houghton Mifflin, 1951), chapter 11; William James, **Psychology—the Briefer Course** (N.Y.: Harper & Row, 1961), chapter 3, "The Self;" Prescott Lecky, Self-Consistency (Garden City, N.Y.: Doubleday, 1958); Ruth C. Wylie, **The Self Concept** (Lincoln, Neb.: University of Nebraska Press, 1961); and "Rogers and Niebuhr," **Pastoral Psychology**, June, 1958, pp. 7-28.

2. See the bibliography for the major works of these prominent "third force" thinkers.

3. Cf. Maslow, **Motivation and Personality** (N.Y.: Harper & Row, 1970), chapter 11.

4. Cf. Fitts, **The Self Concept and Self-Actualization** (Nashville, Tenn.: Counselor Recordings and Tests, 1971), p. 6.

5. Maslow, "Personality Problems and Personality Growth," in Clark E. Moustakas (ed.), **The Self-Explorations in Personal Growth** (N.Y.: Harper Colophon Books, 1974), p. 243.

6. Andras Angyal, "A Theoretical Model for Personality Studies," in Clark E. Moustakas (ed.), **The Self,** pp. 50-51, 54-55.

7. **Motivation and Personality,** p. 101.

8. **Op. cit.,** note 5 **supra,** p. 243.

9. Genesis 1:26, 27.

10. Psalm 8:5.

11. Malachi 2:10.

12. Leviticus 19:2.

13. **The Insecurity of Freedom** (N.Y.: Farrar, Straus, 1966), p. 161.

14. **Who Is Man?** (Stanford, CA.: Stanford University Press, 1965) pp. 46-47.

15. Mishna, Sanhedrin IV:5.

16. Proverbs 14:31.

17. Leviticus 19:18.

18. Avot 2:15.

19. **Ibid.,** 2:18.

20. **Ibid.,** 2:14.

21. **Idem.**

22. "Reinhold Niebuhr and Carl Rogers," **Pastoral Psychology**, June, 1958, p. 18.

23. "Neurosis as a Failure of Growth," **Humanitas,** 1967, p. 166.

24. Mishna, Sanhedrin IV:5.

25. Genesis 18:27.

26. **Man For Himself** (N.Y.: Rinehart & Co., 1947), p. 131. For a similar view see Howard J. Clinebell, Jr., **The Mental Health Ministry of the Church** (Nashville: Abingdon, 1972), pp. 52-3. See also Maslow's discussion of the blurring of the distinction between self and not-self in self-actualizing people, in "A Theory of Metamotivation: The Biological Rooting of the Value-life," in A. J. Sutich and M. A. Vich (eds.), **Readings**

in Humanistic Psychology (N.Y.: The Free Press, 1969), pp. 166-168.

27. Avot 4:4.

28. Ibid., 4:15.

29. Ibid., 1:13.

30. The One Quest (N.Y.: Ballantine Books, 1973), pp. 210-211.

31. The Courage to Be (New Haven: Yale University Press, 1952), p. 157.

32. The Interpersonal Theory of Psychiatry (N.Y.: W. W. Norton, 1953).

33. Talmud, Taanit 23a.

34. Avot 2:5.

35. (N.Y.: Random House, 1972), p. 33.

36. The Greening of America (N.Y.: Bantam Books, 1971), chapters 9 through 12.

37. Cf. "Eupsychia—the Good Society," Journal of Humanistic Psychology, 1:1-11, 1961; Religion, Values and Peak-Experiences (N.Y.: Viking, 1970); "Synergy in the Society and the Individual," Journal of Individual Psychology, 20:153-164; and "Human Potentialities and the Healthy Society," in Herbert Otto (ed.), Human Potentialities (St. Louis: Warren H. Green, 1968).

38. Talmud, Megillah 27b.

39. Talmud, Baba Metzia 58b.

40. Cf. Morris B. Gross, "Jewish Ethics and Self-Psychology," Tradition, Spring, 1959, 1:184-192.

41. Talmud, Ketubot 67b.

42. Midrash on Psalms, ed. S. Buber, p. 284.

43. Talmud, Arachin, 15b.

44. Wiesel, op. cit., p. 69.

45. Articles of Association, Association for Humanistic Psychology, August 28, 1963, quoted in Frank T. Severin (ed.), Humanistic Viewpoints in Psychology (N.Y.: McGraw-Hill, 1965), pp. xv-xvi.

46. "A Theory of Therapy, Personality and Interpersonal Relationships, as Developed in the Client-Centered Framework," in Sigmund Koch (ed.), Psychology: A Study of a Science, Volume III (N.Y.: McGraw-Hill, 1959), pp. 234-235.

47. By "symbolize" Rogers means to become consciously aware of one's experience or to admit that experience into awareness and thereby symbolically represent that experience in a verbal or non-verbal way in his consciousness. See p. 198, op. cit., supra, note 46.

48. John V. Gilmore, The Productive Personality (San Francisco: Albion Pub. Co., 1974), p. 236.

49. "Personality Problems and Personality Growth," pp. 232-233.

50. Cf. Carl R. Rogers, On Becoming a Person (Boston: Houghton Mifflin, 1961), pp. 90-91.

51. Cf. Herbert A. Otto, "New Light on the Human Potential," Saturday Review, December 20, 1969, pp. 14-17.

52. Carl R. Rogers, op. cit., "A Therapist's View of the Good Life: The

Fully Functioning Person," pp. 183-196. Cf. also the Fifteen Propositions of a Holistic Theory of Personality, "Historical Perspective on Holistic Personality Theory," in **Humanistic Psychology: Interviews with Maslow, Murphy, and Rogers,** by Willard B. Frick (Columbus, Ohio: Charles E. Merrill, 1971), pp. 135-138.

53. **The Self—Explorations in Personal Growth** (N.Y.: Harper Colophon Books, 1974), pp. 9-11.

54. "Changes in Relation to Influences upon Self-Conceptualization," **Journal of Abnormal and Social Psychology,** 45:473-480, 1950.

55. For other studies see Don E. Hamachek, **Encounters With the Self** (N.Y.: Holt, Rinehart & Winston, 1971); Wallace D. LaBenne and Bert I. Greene, **Educational Implications of Self-Concept Theory** (Pacific Palisades, Ca.: Goodyear, 1969); and William W. Purkey, **Self-Concept and School Achievement** (Englewood Cliffs, N.Y.: Prentice-Hall, 1970).

56. **The Live Classroom** (N.Y.: Viking Press, 1975), p. 112.

57. "Personal Thoughts on Teaching and Learning," in **On Becoming a Person,** p. 276. Italics original.

58. **Here Comes Everybody** (N.Y.: Harper & Row, Harrow Books, 1972), p. xviii.

59. **Teachers and Learners: The Interactive Process of Education** (Boston: Allyn & Bacon, 1974), p. 13.

60. **Experience and Education** (N.Y.: Macmillan, 1959), esp. chapter 8, "Experience: The Means and Goal of Education."

61. **Annual Handbooks for Group Facilitators** (La Jolla, Ca.: University Associates, 1972, 1973, 1974, 1975, 1976, 1977, 1978); and **Handbook of Structured Experiences for Human Relations Training,** Volumes I-VI (La Jolla, Ca.: University Associates, 1973-1978).

62. John E. Jones and J. William Pfeiffer, **Reference Guide to Handbooks and Annuals** (La Jolla, Ca.: University Associates, 1975), p. 1.

63. **Ibid.,** pp. 1-5.

Chapter 2

RAISING SELF-ESTEEM

Introduction

The Human Potential Movement offers a wide variety of experiential workshops and human relations training events for personal and professional effectiveness. These include communication skills, assertiveness training, conflict resolution, humanizing schools, value clarification, family life education, and others. However, behind the ability to communicate with others, effectively assert oneself, resolve conflicts, and humanize families, schools, and other social systems, is the individual person. The individual is the basic and irreducible unit in all human interaction. Unless the individual is whole and emotionally healthy, all the techniques in the world for effective communication, assertion, etc., will be largely ineffective. Such is our operating assumption.

The self-esteem laboratory is based upon the additional assumption that how one sees oneself is a crucial and dominant factor in personality health. Self-acceptance and self-love are prerequisites for effective functioning and self-actualization. Thus, cognitive understanding and experiential learning in the realm of self concept should be the fundamental building blocks of a program of personal and professional growth.

Goals

It would be foolhardy to believe that a person could permanently alter his self concept in the course of a twenty-four or thirty-six hour workshop (eight or twelve three-hour sessions). But every long trip begins with one step. Raising self-esteem is a life-long process. The self-esteem laboratory initiates a step in this direction. Its goals are to help participants understand the need for self-esteem in effective functioning, to examine one's own self-esteem, to analyze areas which need improvement, and to practice ways of raising self-esteem. It is the presumption of this handbook that once a person tunes himself in to the importance of his self-esteem in daily living, has discovered some effective ways to avoid conditions and circumstances which lower it, and can seek out ways to raise it, he will continue to work on his self-esteem more effectively throughout life. He will also be a more effective change agent in working with others, as parent, teacher, counselor, helper, neighbor, manager, worker and citizen.

It is important not to overstate the goals of a self-esteem workshop. Participants should not be deluded into thinking that a vast and long-range change in their self-esteem will occur by the end of this laboratory experience. It should be made clear that the goals of the lab will be limited to a cognitive understanding of self-esteem and its importance in healthy personality as well as developing a repertoire of methods and tools to monitor and improve one's self-esteem in the back-home atmosphere.

Using This Handbook

This **Handbook** for self-esteem group training is designed to be used by a **trained and experienced group facilitator**. It is not meant as an easy and automatic do-it-yourself kit for someone who has attended an encounter group once and feels ready to be a group trainer. Facilitation of laboratory education demands knowledge, skill, training and experience. Such training should include cognitive and experiential learnings in the fields of child and family development, group dynamics, human relations training, and pedagogy.

The **Handbook** is written to be used selectively and discriminatingly. The trainer using it should know his group, its background and context of personal development. He should have his own clearly formulated and explicitly stated goals. He should be able to draw upon the ideas and conceptions in this **Handbook** to meet his own needs and those of his group.

Self-esteem group training can take place in a school, a church or synagogue, a community center, an industrial setting, a growth center, or in an institution of higher learning. Since its effects will be useful for both personal as well as professional growth, its content is especially appropriate for persons in helping professions, such as teachers, educators, psychologists, counselors, religious leaders, administrators, managers, medical practitioners, and lawyers.

If the self-esteem lab is seen as a beginning, or as one step in a larger plan of personal and professional development which will be reinforced and enriched over longer periods of time, it can have significant effects in the process of helping human beings become more fully functioning persons.

Self Concept Theory

One of the most important developments in understanding human beings in the twentieth century has been our increased understanding of how one's picture of the "self" acts as a crucial factor in achieving personal happiness and effective behavior. More than any other contributor to "self theory" has been Carl Rogers, who has written extensively on the importance of self-esteem in a fully-functioning person.[1] Rogers sees the need of esteem from others and for oneself as an essential starting point for personality health.

Previous schools of psychological thought have emphasized the importance of the influences of one's childhood and repressed fears and guilt on one's psychological health (psychoanalysis). Others have stressed the importance of the environment, both the physical and cultural environment (behaviorism). The school which advocates the "self theory" states that a person lives essentially in his own personal and subjective world.[2] A person's current view of himself, his ability, his appearance, his background, his attitudes and feelings, his goals, all form the picture a person has of himself. This picture, in this viewpoint, is a more important determinant in psychological adjustment and effective behavior than influences of childhood or environmental stimuli. "The self is the star of every performance, the central figure in every act." [3] A person sees the world through the filter of his self, and therefore his view of self will color and influence what he does and does not see, and how he sees that which he does see. The self is the frame of reference for all perception and behavior. It is a window from which the person sees life and the world.

Self Concept and Psychopathology

According to Rogers, when one's experience and one's self concept do not agree, or in his words when there is **incongruence** between self and experience, neurosis develops. The person is unable to symbolize, or become consciously aware of, his experience, because he cannot bear the pain of adjustment of the self concept.[4] The person calls into play his defense mechanisms and screens out his experience. Not being open to this experience, his perception is distorted. The person can no longer be objective. His fears and anxieties interfere with his capacity to think clearly and to adapt to new situations.

Often we meet people who cling to values and attitudes that fly in the face of logic and data in order to preserve their self concept. According to self theorists, all behavior is geared toward maintaining a consistent self concept. Every response to our environment must be in consonance with how we see ourselves. In Rogers' words, "As experiences occur in the life of the individual, they are either symbolized, perceived and organized in some relationship to the self; ignored because there is no perceived relationship to the self structure; denied symbolization or given a distorted symbolization because the experience is inconsistent with the structure of the self." [5]

A person with high self esteem will thus exude confidence, will be open to his experience, and will have the capacity to relate meaningfully to persons and environment. A person with low self-esteem will be fearful of being hurt and will often defend himself by anger, hostility and unproductive behavior. Juvenile delinquents and many kinds of adult malfeasants are persons who think little of themselves, little of others, and maintain a low self-image by acting in accordance with their opinion of themselves. A person's self concept thus acts as a self-fulfilling prophecy. In order to succeed in anything a person has to believe he can succeed. If one sees himself as a failure, he will be one. Self-esteem thus is both the producer and the product of effective behavior, and self-hate is both the producer and the product of ineffective, failing behavior.

Karen Horney offers another suggestion for the origin of low self-esteem.[6] In her practice of psychotherapy she found that people often have inflated, imaginary and unrealistically high images of themselves. To illustrate her point, she describes a cartoon in the **New Yorker** "in which a large middle-aged woman sees herself in the mirror a slender young girl." [7]

Naturally, it is healthy to have high ideals and to strive to be a better person. But the neurotic with an overly-idealized self image is denying his shortcomings, or perhaps condemning them. Instead of his high ideals acting to foster growth and a sense of humility, they act as a hindrance to growth and as a source of arrogance. While authentic ideals are dynamic motivators, over-idealization has a static quality that is not open to modification. [8]

Since a person with an over-idealized self-image can never become that fantasized self, he is constantly exposed to a sense of failure and inadequacy. He thinks ill of himself because he is not reaching his impossible goals. His need to become a saint, a paragon of virtue, forces himself constantly to see himself as a sinner and as the epitome of ineptitude. This low attitude toward self, in turn, produces a person who is highly sensitive to criticism, unable to cope with being blamed, scolded or laughed at, and extremely bothered if others have a low opinion of him. Such a person cannot accept failure with grace, is extremely "touchy" and easily offended. [9]

A person with low self-esteem will frequently retreat into fantasy where he can see himself as he would like to be, avoiding the pain of accepting himself at a level much below his ideal. Or, he may put up a veneer of high confidence and even arrogance, in order to try to convince others that he is worthy. In both of these cases, such a person will have difficulty in interpersonal relationships and thereby foster his sense of isolation and psychological distress. Low self-esteem reinforces itself as it fulfills its own prophecies. [10]

Antecedents of Self-Esteem

A great deal of research has been done in recent years to determine what conditions in child-rearing most frequently lead to helping children develop high self-esteem. [11] Perhaps the best known study in this area is that of Coopersmith [12] who found four conditions most often leading to high self-esteem in children. First, full acceptance of the child by his parents. (This would correspond with Rogers' description of the need for unconditional positive regard). [13] Second, clearly defined and enforced limits. This has the effect of giving the child a basis for evaluating his performance in terms of expectations and taboos of parents and community. It also provides high standards of performance which are usually met. Third, respect for the child as a person and willingness to take his wishes and needs into serious consideration. The child is not a pawn to be maneuvered and manipulated, nor a servant to act upon the command of a dictatorial parent. Parents with children having high self-esteem are willing to negotiate family rules within carefully drawn limits. They also have less needs for punitive discipline, more often reward positive behavior than disapprove of negative behavior. Such parents show their positive regard through availability for discussion, taking an interest in the child's friends and in his or her social and academic life generally. Fourth, a high level of self-esteem in parents. It seems obvious that parents with high self-esteem can fulfill the other three requirements, of full acceptance, establishing limits and standards, and extending respect for children as worthwhile human beings.

From a negative viewpoint, Angyal [14] states that in neurotic development there are always circumstances which instill in the child a feeling of worthlessness. A healthy personality must have the feeling of being competent and lovable. The neurotic feels inadequate to master the situations that face him and undeserving of love. Some of the factors which bring about a feeling of being incompetent and unlovable are: overprotective parents who do so much for the child that he gets a message of being incapable of doing for himself;excessive criticism which creates a feeling of "I can't do anything right;" exaggerated praise which creates standards impossible to reach and subsequent feelings of worthlessness; too many "don'ts" which make a child feel that everything he does is sinful and evil; and lack of fundamental respect for the child as a person which gives him the feeling of being unimportant and worthless. The end result is a child who feels incapable and unlovable.

Coopersmith finds that treatment associated with high self-esteem "is much more vigorous, active, and contentious than is the case in families that produce children with low self-esteem. Rather than being a paradigm of tranquillity, harmony and open-mindedness, we find that the high self-esteem family is notable for the high level of activity of its individual members, strong-minded parents dealing with independent, assertive, children, stricter enforcement of more stringent demands, and greater possibilities for open dissent and disagreement. This picture brings to mind firm convictions, frequent and possibly strong exchanges, and people who are capable and ready to assume leadership and who will not be treated casually or disrespectfully. [15]

Raising Self-Esteem

According to Maslow [16] self-esteem is established through respect and approval from others, actual achievement and success, and acceptance of and acting upon one's inner nature.

Learning to accept oneself is a key building block in the structure of self-esteem. One realistically assesses abilities and capitalizes on strengths while recognizing weaknesses. High self-esteem is not predicated upon total success. It means a readiness to see in oneself those limitations that are there, and a healthy sense of pride in the abilities and competencies that are present. It also implies a trust of one's inner nature, the ability to make decisions confidently, and carry them out even in the face of disapproval and criticism.

The utilitization of one's potential can be achieved in many ways. Setting goals, making contracts, and risking new behaviors are several ways. Participants in a self-esteem lab can be encouraged to try new things, to expand the limits of their self concept, and to take reasonable risks in order to reach greater adequacy and competence as a human being. Since interpersonal relationships are among the most significant areas of personal effectiveness, the atmosphere of trust and intimacy in a human relations laboratory can provide an ideal atmosphere for experimentation in developing new interpersonal skills.

However, the basic thrust of the self-esteem laboratory is the first of Maslow's three roads to healthy self-esteem—namely, approval from others, or, as we call it, affirmation and validation. A fuller elaboration of the affirmation model will be given in chapter 3 of this **Handbook.** Suffice it to say here that experiences of giving and receiving sincere, deserved approvoal from individuals and the group will encourage a person's revising his self-image.

Stress should be placed on the idea that one's self concept is learned and, therefore, can be changed. It is built, in Sullivan's phrase, upon "reflected appraisals" of significant others.[17] Parents, family members, teachers, authority figures, friends, all contribute to one's self image. The person assimilates the views of others and they become his views.

While one's self image becomes fairly fixed by approximately age seven, it can always be changed and modified. Every positive and affirming behavior by another to oneself is a contribution, however slight, toward raising one's self-esteem. One's self-esteem rises and falls, within given parameters, throughout one's life. No one has a rigid and totally unchangeable evaluation of self. By receiving warmth, respect, love and affirmation, a person can grow in self-acceptance and self-love. Thus, most of the structured experiences that comprise the heart of the self-esteem laboratory are designed to affirm and validate the essential goodness and humanness of the participants.

The self-esteem laboratory is strength- and health-oriented, rather than pathology-oriented. It stresses the recognition of strengths rather than the removal of weaknesses. It encourages participants to cease discounting the love and approval of others, and to learn how to "take in" the positive strokes from the community of learners. It attempts to build a healthy community where approval of self and others is acceptable and commendable, and where intimate relationships and sharing of love and affection are fostered and encouraged. It seeks to establish an atmosphere in which each person present can experience the essential goodness of his being and help others to do the same; in which all strive together to fan the divine spark within into a glowing flame, and bask in the ultimate approvoal and affirmation of the Source of all Being.

FOOTNOTES

1. Cf. **On Becoming a Person** (Boston: Houghton Mifflin, 1961), and **Client-Centered Therapy** (Boston: Houghton Mifflin, 1951).
2. Rogers, "A Theory of Therapy, Personality, and Interpersonal Relationships, as Developed in the Client-Centered Framework," in S. Koch (ed.), **Psychology: A Study of a Science,** Volume 3 (New York: McGraw-Hill, 1959), p. 191.
3. A. W. Combs, D. L. Avila and William W. Purkey, **Helping Relationships** (Boston: Allyn and Bacon, 1971), p. 39.
4. **Op. cit.,** in note 2, **supra,** pp. 234-5.
5. **Client-Centered Therapy** (Boston: Houghton Mifflin, 1951), p. 503.
6. **Our Inner Conflicts** (N.Y.: W. W. Norton, 1945), chapter 6, "The Idealized Image," pp. 96-114.
7. **Ibid.,** p. 96.
8. **Ibid.,** pp. 98-99.
9. Morris Rosenberg, **Society and the Adolescent Self-Image** (Princeton, New Jersey: Princeton University Press, 1965), p. 158.
10. **Ibid.,** pp. 161-167.
11. Cf. Don E. Hamacheck, **Encounters With the Self** (N.Y.: Holt, Rinehart and Winston, 1971), chapter 5, "Self-Concept as Related to Child-Rearing Practices," pp. 131-173, and references cited there.
12. Stanley Coopersmith, **The Antecedents of Self-Esteem** (San Francisco: W. H. Freeman, 1967), pp. 235-263.
13. **Op. cit.,** note 2 **supra,** pp. 224, 230, 234.
14. "A Theoretical Model for Personality Studies," in Clark E. Moustakas (ed.), **The Self—Explorations in Personal Growth** (N.Y.: Harper Colophon Books, 1956), p. 51.
15. **Op. cit.,** pp. 252-3.
16. "Personality Problems and Personality Growth," in Clark E. Moustakas (ed.), **The Self—Explorations in Personal Growth** (New York: Harper Colophon Books, 1974), p. 243.
17. Harry Stack Sullivan, **The Interpersonal Theory of Psychiatry** (New York: W. W. Norton, 1953).

FOR FURTHER READING

Dorothy C. Briggs, **Your Child's Self-Esteem.** Garden City, N.Y.: Doubleday, Dolphin Booke, 1975.

William H. Fitts, et al. **The Self Concept and Self-Actualization.** Nashville, Tenn.: Counselor Recordings and Tests, 1971.

Haim G. Ginott, **Between Parent and Child.** N.Y.: Avon Books, 1969.

Don E. Hamachek, **Encounters with the Self.** New York: Holt, Rinehart and Winston, 1971.

Thomas A. Harris, **I'm OK, You're OK.** New York: Harper & Row, 1967.

Maxwell Maltz, **The Magic Power of Self-Image Psychology.** New York: Pocket Books, 1970.

Virginia Satir, **Peoplemaking.** Palo Alto, Calif.: Science and Behavior Books, 1972.

Bill and Carole Tegeler, **The People Press—Life Script Awareness.** La Jolla, Ca.: University Associates, 1975.

Kaoru Yamamoto, **The Child and His Image.** Boston: Houghton Mifflin, 1972.

Chapter 3

THE AFFIRMATION MODEL

"Praise is the sweetest of all sounds"—Cicero.

The assumption upon which the self-esteem lab is designed is that a person's self concept is a crucial factor in personality health if not the most important factor. Certainly it is a prerequisite for personal adjustment, personality growth, self-actualization, positive relationships, and productive, creative and zestful living.[1] The basic need for positive regard from others and self is, in Rogers' words, "universal," "pervasive and persistent."[2]

A person with low self-esteem is blocked in his ability to perceive and accurately symbolize his experiences in his awareness. Because of his need for self-regard he interprets experiences in a manner consistent with his perception of himself. Inaccurate symbolization of his experiences leads to inability to organize his experiences into his self-structure in an accurately symbolized form.[3]

Early experiences of "I'm not O.K." thus tend to cripple a person's ability to be open to his experience in a way that will make him happy, rational and vital. Illusions, fantasies, false information, and magical and irrational thinking, all prevent such a person from growth choices and decisions and foster in their place defense choices and decisions.

If persons have a basic need for positive regard from others and self, how is it that they are deprived of such regard? Claude Steiner[4] suggests that parents use positive regard as a weapon with which to control their children's lives. Basic training in life for most people consists of **conditional regard** rather than unconditional regard. "Be a good boy, and Mommy will love you," is the message the child receives. The obvious conclusion which follows is "If you are naughty, Mommy will not love you." Out of such a conditional psychological environment, it is hard for a child to accept a notion of "I'm O.K."

The effects of withholding strokes and unconditional positive regard are disastrous for the growing personality. Says Steiner:[5]

In **Games People Play**, speaking about stimulus hunger, Berne says: "A biological chain may be postulated leading from emotional and sensory deprivation through apathy to degenerative changes and death. In this sense stimulus hunger has the same relationship to survival of the human organism as food hunger." The notion that strokes are, throughout a person's life, as indispensable as food is a notion that has not been sufficiently emphasized. Therefore, I wish to restate the fact: **strokes are as necessary to human life as are other primary biological needs such as the need for food, water, and shelter—needs which, if not satisfied, will lead to death.**

As Berne pointed out in the chapter on strokes in **Transactional Analysis in Psychotherapy**, control of stimulation is far more effective in manipulating human behavior than brutality or punishment. Thus, while a few families still use brutality in an attempt to control their offspring, most injunctions are enforced in young persons through the manipulation of strokes rather than through physical punishment.

Not only do parents frequently withhold strokes and positive regard for manipulative purposes, but they also frequently denigrate and demean their children with name-calling, stressing of weaknesses or expressions of lack of trust. The lasting effects of this kind of negative behavior toward children are well known. Even those who have later grown and become more self-actualized in their mature years frequently retain the negative effects of being put-down by parents, teachers and other significant persons. [6]

An example of such a case is Fritz Perls, founder of Gestalt Therapy. His wife, Laura, described the effects on Fritz of being put down constantly by his father and the results of that treatment in his later life: [7]

Fritz had a carry-over of his father's attitude toward him, which was always denigrating. His father called him a "piece of shit," which was terrible. If I did anything it was to counteract that—to give him a feeling, or get him to the point where he could get a feeling of his own worth. But when I said anything that was at all critical, he felt completely devastated. As if I was calling him "no good." And I certainly never did. Not even at the time when he was most hostile and rejecting.

Abraham Maslow goes one step further in saying that not only do parent-child relationships have the potential for nurturing healthy personalities, but within every relationship are the seeds for either growth or sickness. "Let people realize clearly," he stated, "that every time they threaten someone or humiliate or hurt unnecessarily or dominate or reject another human being, they become forces for the creation of psychopathology, even if these be small forces. Let them recognize that every man who is kind, helpful, decent, psychologically democratic, affectionate, and warm, is a psychotherapeutic force even though a small one." [8]

The Need for Affirmation

The patterns of child-rearing described by Steiner have lead to wide-spread loss of self-esteem among the majority of persons today. Psychotherapists report that most of their patients suffered loss of self-esteem in their developmental years. Hence, methods of restoring one's sense of positive self-regard, of "I'm O.K.", is a crucial task for persons in psychology, education, religion and other related disciplines.

The fundamental assumption of the self-esteem lab is that persons may regain a high self-esteem even though they may not presently enjoy such good feelings about themselves. The major approach in the self-esteem lab is the **affirmation model.**

Persons who have been deprived of limitless stroking in order to manipulate their behavior, and any person whose significant others during the growing-up years deprived him, for whatever reason, of the necessary supply of love, attention, stroking, unconditional positive regard and affirmation, will be helped through being affirmed in his present existence.

According to Rogers, in order to help a person become less defensive and more open to accurately perceive and symbolize experience—that is, to be a rational, confident and loving person—"There must be an increase in unconditional self-regard." Furthermore, this can come about through the "communicated unconditional positive regard of a significant other...." [9]

Martin Buber sees the need for affirmation, or confirmation, of one person to another, as a crucial element in human encounter. [10]

The basis of man's life with man is two fold, and it is one—the wish of every man to be confirmed as what he is, even as what he can become, by men; and the innate capacity in man to confirm his fellowmen in this way.... Genuine conversation...means acceptance of otherness.... (Everything) depends, so far as human life is concerned, on whether each thinks of the other as the one he is (and) ...unreservedly accepts and confirms him in his being this man and in his being made in this particular way....

Man wishes to be confirmed in his being by man, and wishes to have a presence in the being of the other.... Secretly and bashfully he watches for a Yes which allows him to be and which can come to him only from one human person to another.

The Affirmation Model

The basic thrust of the self-esteem lab is **affirmation.** Each person is given opportunities to affirm other participants. One is also given opportunities to affirm oneself. Besides these experiential learnings, some discussion should take place about the nature of nurturing human beings, as parents, teachers, counselors, and other helpers, skilled and unskilled. [11] Stress should be placed here upon the need for **unconditional positive regard,** transmitted in a context of emphathic understanding, [12] as a source for facilitating the development of positive self concepts and raising a low self concept.

In the context of the self-esteem lab, an atmosphere of empathy and unconditional positive regard should be fostered as much as possible. Gerald Jud's notion that love is **intentional** and **not time-bound** is important. [13] In other words, persons can **choose** to love each other, and accept each other fully as human beings with all their faults, and can achieve this love in a very short period of time, even within the course of a weekend.

Within that kind of atmosphere, there is repeated emphasis on the strengths and positive traits of the participants. Even while accepting others unconditionally, our acceptance and positive regard for them fosters within us a desire to help them recognize their own assets, strengths and positive qualities. This is the basis of the structured experiences of validation and affirmation of selves and others.

Studies in counselor effectiveness have shown that effective therapy takes place most often when the therapist stresses the client's **strengths** rather than his weaknesses. Studying recorded sessions of psychotherapy of over fifty different therapists, Berenson, Mitchel and Laney discovered that effective helpers use "confrontations of strength" much more frequently than "confrontations of weakness." [14]

The presumption in the affirmation model is that a person has enough strengths and resources, if one is capable of marshalling them and utilizing them, to overcome one's own weakness and correct one's own false perceptions and illusions, closing the gap between the ideal and real self. The goal of therapy and skill training would be, therefore, to stress a person's strengths and resources, to point out what these are, and to facilitate the ability to recognize and acknowledge these within oneself.

In the self-esteem lab various structured experiences help participants affirm and validate themselves and others. A first century Hindu scriptural poem summarizes the approach of the affirmation model:[15]

> Oh, let the self exalt itself,
> Not sink itself below;
> Self is the only friend of self,
> And self self's only foe.
> For self, when it subdues itself
> Befriends itself. And so
> When it eludes self-conquest, is
> Its own and only foe.
> So calm, so self-subdued, the self
> Has an unshaken base
> Through pain and pleasure, cold and heat
> Through honor and disgrace.

Herbert Otto, Director of the National Center for the Exploration of Human Potential, in La Jolla, California, believes that praise and affirmation are important in helping people regain contact with their own strengths, recources and potentialities.[16] He writes:[17]

> Everyone is starved for the deserved recognition and praise which should come with a job well done. In our pathology and problem-centered culture, the emphasis is continually on the deficiencies, the shortcomings, the mistakes, and the inadequacies of people. Yet psychological tests with children have clearly revealed that when tired children were given a word of praise or commendation, an upward surge of new energy was evident. (An endless number of cases can be cited where the praise and encouragement of the child by his teacher has significantly influenced his course and development in life.) Conversely, when children were criticized or discouraged, their available physical energy declined dramatically.
>
> As the noted psychologist Erik Erikson has pointed out, the ego identity of children "gains real strength only from whole-hearted and consistent recognition of real accomplishment." This also applies to adults. A considerable number of psychological studies indicate that if adult subjects in experiments are rewarded by praise and commendation, their performance significantly improves as judged by themselves and by others, and gains are evident in leadership, participation, and self confidence....

Potential Pitfalls of the Affirmation Model

As in all techniques, the affirmation model can be abused and misused. Instead of pointing out strengths and resources in others and acknowledging them in ourselves, this model can become license for mindless sweetness, undeserved praise and sugary but superficial compliments. How do we distinguish between true affirmation, of which Martin Buber spoke, and hollow compliments?

There are criteria for effective affirmation-giving:

1) **Sincerity.** One does not need to invent or exaggerate in giving praise and commendation. This will surely have the opposite effect. Carl Struever, a teacher of Re-Evaluation Counseling, in which the Affirmation Model is frequently employed, wrote this in a recent R. C. newsletter: "In any validation we make it sincere. You search in your reaction to the other person, to yourself, for validation that you regard as true. Some glimpse or sign of your real self. You are armed with the understanding about the real person and the distress pattern co-existing, so you have a way to understand the surface paradox of the dumb things you do vs. realization that you are a good and competent person. Both have been happening. You are training the beam of your attention radar on the real person, instead of where it was: on the distress."[18]

Sincerity also implies that the praise and commendation is not a condition for positive regard. One might say, "I felt warm towards you when you danced with me so gracefully," rather than "You are a great dancer, I really like you." Positive regard should be **unconditional** and the giving of praise and appreciation is independently and freely given. The relationship should not be viewed as depending on the continuation of the skill or ability being admired and commended.

Sincerity also implies that a compliment is not manipulative; that is, in order to persuade someone to do something we want, or to like us more. It also means that praise should be free-standing, and not the prelude to a criticism. People are often so accustomed to the "I like you **but**...." that they frequently cannot hear the praise preceding the put-down.[19]

2) The person praised should try to **acknowledge** the strengths and resources found in him, especially if these are checked out sufficiently with several people, such as group members. A common tendency among people is to "flick back" a compliment as soon as they receive one, or deny it or discount it in some way.

Claude Steiner explains how this is often done:[20]

Jack may find that he is not aware of many, if any, good things about himself and that he is incapable of using words which imply goodness or worth applied to him. If anyone attempts to supply strokes, he will reject some, most, or all of the strokes with a discount.

If someone says, "You have beautiful skin," the Parent says, internally, "They haven't seen you up close." If someone says, "You have a lovely smile," the Parent says, "But they haven't seen you angry." If a person says, "You're very intelligent," then the Parent says, "Yes, but you're ugly." Other devices to avoid the acceptance of strokes will be observed, such as: giving token acceptance of the stroke, followed by a shrug so that the stroke will roll off the shoulders instead of "soaking in"; or immediately reciprocating with a counter stroke which essentially says, "I don't deserve a stroke so I must give one in return." Another argument against taking strokes is, "These people don't know you, their strokes have got to be phony." This, in spite of the fact that everyone may have agreed to give only sincere, genuine strokes.

Of course, after accepting and acknowledging the praise, the recipient should then be capable of continuing to fulfill that praise and commendation with even greater vigor and enthusiasm. Total integration of the unrecognized (or under-recognized) strength should eventually follow the good feelings about oneself resulting from praise and affirmation. Along with that should be acceptance of the fact that the person may not be able to act upon every strength newly recognized by self or others. Self-acceptance of where one is should also be wedded with the search for newer and greater strengths and their implementation and integration.

Remembering that the ultimate purpose of validation and affirmation is integration of strengths into the total self will help avoid the idea that too much praise is damaging and corrupting. The opposite is really the case. Sidney Simon, who is active in the use of the affirmation model in education and growth groups, states, "I don't know anyone who walks around suffering from too much validation." [21] Harvey Jackins, founder of Re-evaluation Counseling, one of the leading proponents of the affirmation model, suggests that self-affirmation should be done vigorously and without reservations. Only then will the person be able to overcome past patterns of self-criticism and constant put-downs. He writes: [22]

The more enthusiastic the self-approval (the client) attempts, the more his mind is invaded by the "fruit bats" of self-doubt, self-criti-cism, suddenly remembered and apparently genuine flaws in his char-acter and the whole miserable record of his apparent past failures and short-comings. These, of course, are just the recordings out of which the chronic pattern of non-survival behavior was built. To the client, however, they tend to seem more and more brilliantly logical and ac-curate than his previous logical commitment to unlimited self-approv-al. His commitment to self-approval begins to appear to be ridiculous, mistaken fantasy which he has just matured away from in the last few minutes.

To keep the process working, however, he need remember only one thing, that is, to stick by his guns and keep expressing unlimited self-approval in words, tone of voice, posture and facial expression.

3) **Appreciative vs. Evaluative Praise.** Haim Ginott differentiates between **appreciative** praise and **evaluative** praise.[23] He points out correctly that judgmental praise, the kind a boss gives an employee, "creates anxiety, invites dependency, and evokes defensiveness." This kind of praise is paternalistic and condescending. It might sound like this

(imagine a deep, knowing tone of voice): "Good job, Watson, keep up the good work."

To avoid sounding supercilious and judgmental, Ginott makes several suggestions:

(1) "In praising appreciate specific acts. Do not evaluate character traits." To a child who returned lost money, one should not say, "How honest you are!" but rather, "Thank you for finding the money. You saved Andrea much sorrow."

(2) "Avoid praise that attaches adjectives to a (person's) character." Instead of saying "You're a great guy," one might say, "I feel good towards you when you help people."

(3) "Only praise that does not judge the (person's) character or evaluate his personality makes it safe for him to err without fear and to recover without anxiety." Instead of saying "You have a perfect eye," the praiser might say: "Your arrow hit the bull's eye."

(4) "The cardinal rule in praising is: Describe without evaluating. Report—don't judge. Leave the evaluation of the (person) to him." Instead of saying "You are a super artist," say "I like the colorful way you draw. It makes me feel warm." The emphasis is on self-disclosure of feelings and thoughts, not on judging the other or evaluating his character.

Summary

The Affirmation Model has great potential for reforming persons, institutions and communities. It is easy to envisage families, schools, business, countries and governments, in which a sense of personal affection, wholesome personal relationships, and productive activity take place. With persons who have high self-esteem, and who affirm and confirm other human beings constantly, such a healthy synergistic society is possible.

I can testify personally to the effects which affirmation exercises and experiences have had on my own personal happiness and self-esteem. While at first I thought such compliments would be phony and useless, I found them to be effective confrontations to my former patterns of self-put-downs. I have also found that I have warmer and fuller relationships with those around me whom I can affirm and validate frequently.

Part of the reservations we have stems from cultural taboos, such as the fear of homosexuality which prevents stroking between persons of the same sex; the fear of moral improprieties which prevents stroking between married persons of the opposite sex; and the fear of seemingly inappropriate intimacy between persons of different generations who are not of the same nuclear family. As Claude Steiner puts it, "The free exchange of strokes is a managed activity, a situation in which the means of satisfaction of a basic need are made unavailable to people." [24]

"The end result is that the capacity to love is taken away from people and then directed against them by using it as a reinforcer to bring about desired behavior." [24]

Gestalt therapists Erving and Miriam Polster have found the use of affirmation, even when it would seem on the surface that the affirmation is unwarranted, to be one of the most "exciting and warming exercises" used by them in large groups. [25]

A person comes to the center of the group, says his name, and the group applauds and cheers for a full minute while he acknowledges the applause in whatever way he feels. On the face of it this sounds like a phony maneuver. It is contrived, of course, since the person hasn't **done** anything to merit the applause. Nevertheless, in almost every instance the applause is experienced as altogether right, even spontaneous and genuine, and moreover it is a mind-blowing delight for both the applauders and the applauded. It is a momentary engagement of love, with nothing to gain but joy. We are profoundly in need of love statements but we have trained ourselves well not to make them except with our intimates, and even then only in "right" moments.

FOOTNOTES

1. William H. Fitts et al, **The Self Concept and Self-Actualization** (Nashville, Tenn.: Counselor Recordings and Tests, 1971). This book is Monograph III of a series of seven called "Studies on the Self Concept."

2. "A Theory of Personality," in Theodore Millon, **Theories of Psychopathology and Personality** (Philadelphia: W. B. Saunders, 1973), p. 218.

3. **Ibid.,** pp. 220-221.

4. "The Stroke Economy," in Claude Steiner, ed., **Readings in Radical Psychiatry** (New York: Grove Press, 1975), pp. 28-9.

5. **Loc. cit.**

6. Cf. Lou Benson, **Images, Heroes and Self-Perceptions,** chapter 3, "The Put-Down," (Englewood Cliffs, New Jersey: Prentice-Hall, 1974), pp. 45-76.

7. Quoted in **Fritz** by Martin Shepard (New York: E. P. Dutton, 1975), p. 72.

8. **Motivation and Personality** (New York: Harper and Row, 1970), p. 254.

9. **Op. cit.,** note 2 **supra,** p. 223.

10. **The Knowledge of Man** (New York: Harper and Row, 1965), pp. 67-71. See also the dialog between Buber and Carl Rogers (pp. 181-2) which makes a fine distinction between Buber's "confirmation" and Rogers' "acceptance."

11. See two excellent volumes of A. W. Combs, D. L. Avila and W. W. Purkey, **Helping Relationships** (Boston: Allyn and Bacon, 1971), and **The Helping Relationship Sourcebook** (Boston: Allyn and Bacon, 1971).

12. Rogers, **op. cit.,** p. 223.

13. **Training in the Art of Loving** (Philadelphia: Pilgrim Press, 1972), p. 24.

14. "Level of Therapist Functioning, Types of Confrontation and Type of Patient," **Journal of Clinical Psychology,** 1968, 24:111-113. Cf. J. Douds, B. G. Berenson, R. R. Carkhuff, and Richard Pierce, "In search of an honest experience: Confrontation in counseling and life," in R. R. Carkhuff and B. G. Berenson, eds., **Beyond Counseling and Therapy,** (New York: Holt, Rinehart and Winston, 1967), pp. 170-179; and Robert R. Kurtz and John E. Jones, "Confrontation: Types, Conditions, and Outcomes," in J. Jones and J. W. Pfeiffer, eds., **The 1973 Annual Handbook for Group Facilitators** (La Jolla, Ca.: University Associates, 1973), pp. 135-8.

15. Quoted in W. D. La Benne and B. I. Greene, **Educational Implications of Self-Concept Theory.** (Pacific Palisades, Ca.: Goodyear, 1969), p. 1.

16. Cf. H. A. Otto, **A Guide to Developing Your Potential,** (No. Hollywood, Ca.: Wilshire Book Co., 1974).

17. Quoted in Frank Goble, **The Third Force** (New York: Pocket Books, 1971), pp. 156-7.

18. Mimeographed newsletter, n. d., p. 4.

19. Cf. Richard E. Farson, "Praise Reappraised," **Harvard Business**

Review, September-October, 1963, and Sally W. Olds, "Why Compliments Make You Uneasy," **Today's Health,** February, 1975, pp. 24-27.

20. **Scripts People Live** (New York: Grove Press, 1974), p. 116. By "Parent," Steiner means, of course, the person's Parent ego state (of T. A.'s Parent-Adult-Child ego states), not the person's actual parent.

21. Quoted by Olds, p. 27 (see note 19).

22. "The Complete Appreciation of Oneself," in Harvey Jackins, **The Human Situation** (Seattle: Rational Island Publishers, 1973), pp. 44-56. (Quotation cited is found on pp. 52-3).

23. **Teacher and Child** (New York: Avon Books, 1975), chapter 5, "The Perils of Praise," pp. 101-116.

24. **Op. Cit.** (note 20), pp. 116-117.

25. **Gestalt Therapy Integrated** (New York: Vintage Books, 1974), pp. 304-5.

FOR FURTHER READING

Lou Benson, **Images, Heroes and Self-Perceptions.** Englewood Cliffs, New Jersey: Prentice-Hall, 1974.

Stanley Coopersmith, **The Antecedents of Self-Esteem.** San Francisco: W. H. Freeman and Co., 1967.

_____, "Studies in Self-Esteem," **Scientific American,** February, 1968, pp. 96-106.

William H. Fitts, et. al. **The Self Concept and Self-Actualization.** Nashville, Tenn.: Counselor Recordings and Tests, 1971.

Erich Fromm, **The Art of Loving.** New York: Harper and Row, 1956.

Haim G. Ginott, **Teacher and Child.** New York: Avon Books, 1972.

Milton Mayeroff, **On Caring.** New York: Harper and Row, 1971.

Virginia Satir, **Peoplemaking.** Palo Alto, Ca.: Science and Behavior Books, 1972.

Claude Steiner, **Scripts People Live.** New York: Grove Press 1974.

Bill and Carole Tegeler, **The People Press.** La Jolla, Ca.: University Associates, 1975.

Kaoru Yamamoto, **The Child and His Image.** Boston(Houghton Mifflin, 1972.

Chapter 4

THE AUTHOR'S SELF-ESTEEM

Leaders of a self-esteem lab should pay special attention to their own self-esteem so that they can illustrate points in the course of the workshop from their own personal experience. Mini-lectures, processing of structured experiences, and answers to group members' questions can all gain strength, relevance and authenticity through punctuating the remarks with a personal example. To do this it will be necessary for the group facilitator to be especially aware of how his own self-esteem has risen and fallen in the past and how it continues to do so.

One good technique for increasing self-awareness in the area of self-esteem is taking the time to write out a history of one's self-esteem. Paying attention to one's thoughts, feelings, body changes, emotional reactions, are an important part of personal growth. Fritz Perls and the Gestalt therapists who followed him considered awareness to be the key to increased personality health.[1] It certainly is a significant aspect of being a competent and facilitative group leader. Taking the time to write out one's own personal history in the area of self-esteem will heighten this requisite awareness.

In the history one should take special note of factors in one's life which helped produce high self-esteem and those which helped reduce one's self-esteem, especially during the developing years. One should also pay close attention to the thoughts, feelings, behaviors and activities which bring on higher and lower self-esteem in one's present life.

A trainer might consider presenting a history of his own self-esteem as an introduction to a self-esteem workshop, or at some later point. This will serve several purposes.

1) present an example of self-disclosure, an attitude and behavior which the trainer wants to model as early and as often as possible during the workshop;

2) give a personal example of how self-awareness in the area of self-esteem has contributed to one person's personal growth, productivity and happiness;

3) help group members realize that even the leader is still working on problems of self-esteem since the enhancement of self-image is a life-long process;

4) help create a safe and non-threatening atmosphere in which openness and authenticity are the hallmarks;

5) provide a convenient way to open the workshop in a personal, meaningful, open fashion.

To provide a sample of how one might write a history of his self-esteem, I shall present a brief outline of some of the highlights of my own. This is meant merely to provide a few examples of factors which have helped or harmed my own self-esteem. It is by no means meant to portray a comprehensive picture of the development and growth of my self image.

Personal History

A source of high self-esteem in my primary family was the loving devotion of my mother, a mature, very intelligent and an extremely devoted parent. She had tenderness and strength. She complimented me, praised me, validated me often, took a great interest in my school work, my extra-curricular activities and my social life—all without imposing her will or being domineering. She made me feel like a lovable, capable, worthwhile person.

My father was a good and loving person, hard working, with high ethical values. However, he was sometimes emotionally inadequate, finding it difficult to express feelings, especially during my growing-up years. He was often withdrawn and did not reach out emotionally either to my mother or my older brother or myself. I was never aware of feeling rejected by him, but I did sometimes feel that my friends' fathers took a greater interest in their lives and that made me feel unimportant.

My brother, four years older, was more physically-oriented and had a stronger constitution. I often felt inadequate in comparison with him, since I saw myself as skinny and weaker. I had frequent colds, was allergic to several kinds of foods, would break out in hives, and saw myself as being unmasculine and, therefore, in many ways inadequate. I was never challenged by parents or teachers to develop my body or physical skills and never took an interest in active or spectator sports. When friends would play rough contact sports or engage in conversation about professional sports, I felt inadequate. My brother frequently looked upon me as a baby and either roughed me up or ignored me. What I now see as a common sibling pattern was perceived by me then as due to my inadequacy, physical weakness and lack of masculinity and maturity. These experiences were often sources of low self-esteem.

My intellectual capacities became a source of high self-esteem in most of my growing-up years. In later elementary school grades and after, I could only interest myself in certain subject areas, and in those I did extremely well: language arts and mathematics. In history and geography I did only fairly. Positive feedback on my good grades were always boosts to my self-esteem, while my failures brought down my self-esteem.

I always liked my physical appearance (even though not my physical weakness and undeveloped potentialities). I had a well-shaped body and handsome face. I remember often staring at myself in the mirror, narcissus-like. This often compensated in my fantasy world for weakness in sports and sometimes in social interaction. My being pleased with my appearance was a source of high self-esteem for me. I would constantly receive positive strokes for my appearance and that compensated for put-downs in other area. Whenever I felt down, I could look at myself in the mirror and get pleasure. However, relying on that one aspect of my total self, as an escape and a way to avoid taking positive action to improve other parts of me, prevented me from attempting to change the undeveloped parts. In other words, my pleasant appearance served both as a source of high self-esteem and at the same time as a defense which served ultimately as a source of low self-esteem.

I always had a few close friends and felt good about that. I was especially successful in the area of boy-girl relationships, as early as fifth grade. In my teenage, dating years, I always had the most sought-after female companions, which helped my self-image.

I always possessed a special sensitivity to people's feelings and was looked upon as a warm, understanding person, and a friend to whom people could talk with ease and trust. Having many people come to me and share their problems with me was always good for my ego.

In task groups, youth, social and cultural groups, high school study clubs and other informal social-cultural structures, I was a popular leader, being intelligent, articulate and possessing distinct leadership traits. Attaining positions of high office, organizing and implementing many important projects and activities, helped me see myself as a highly competent, bright and effective leader.

I was recognized for my intelligence and leadership traits particularly in my religious congregation. There I flowered as a leader who could do public speaking with ease, write articles and speeches for myself and others, and always shined in public performances and other appearances. Audience applause, letters of commendation, and personal validations were very meaningful to me, and were constant boosts to my self-esteem.

Being a Jew was a great source of pride, happiness and high sense of self-importance. I was part of a special, unique, and very gifted people—a tiny minority which made untold contributions to human civilization. My pride as a Jew was always a boost for my pride in my total self. On the other hand, an occasional experience of anti-Semitism sometimes caused me to think that I was part of a "pushy, money-grabbing" race of people. Not often, but on occasion I would internalize the stereotypes of the majority culture, causing me to feel some degree of self-hatred and shame. Fortunately, most of my experiences with being Jewish, such as family holiday celebrations and pleasant educational experiences in religious school and informal youth programs, were positive and constructive and these far outweighed the negative experiences.

In my professional career as a rabbi, educator, writer and public speaker, I have received extremely high honors and recognition, giving me a deep sense of happiness and fulfillment, constantly a source of high self-esteem.

Ways I Lower and Raise My Self-Esteem

Despite a plethora of positive traits, positive and loving child-rearing from my parents, some of my negative childhood experiences continue to exist in my phenomenal world to bring on feelings of low self-esteem and lack of self-confidence.

At age 31 I began to take better care of my physical health, eating carefully, watching my weight, exercising, and looking and feeling trim and fit. Activity in tennis and jogging are now a more regular part of my weekly routine. These have helped me recapture my sense of masculinity and physical fitness.

My childhood narcissism persisted in many ways, preventing me from paying attention to other people and often being self-centered in social and professional relationships. I have made progress in this area, but have some way to go yet, too. Individual psychotherapy was the most effective growth experience in beginning to overcome this inadequacy.

Another contributing factor in my low self-esteem was my perception of my father's neglect and my perceptions of my brother's treatment towards me. I constantly find myself compulsively striving for perfection and high levels of productivity in my professional life to gain the strokes from the world which I wanted from my father and brother as a child. Being more aware of these needs helps me overcome them, but not completely.

I have a number of patterns which bring instant low self-esteem. One is making comparisons with other people. I often find myself having a need to be the very best, and to be in control, in every group of which I am a part. When I pay attention to the feeling of inadequacy which this brings me, I realize what I am doing to myself and, becoming more rational and realistic, the feel of inadequacy disappears. I am finding more and more that **self-awareness** and **self-acceptance** are two major keys for me for high self-esteem.

Another source of low self-esteem is my unrealistic ideal self. I have extremely high standards of behavior and performance for myself. When I do not meet these immediately, I feel inadequate. When I am able to reflect on the images I have created for myself, and understand how unrealistic they often are, I find that I am much more self-accepting.

If I find myself quiet or withdrawn in a group of people, I begin to think that I am socially inadequate and not out-going enough. At such times I have begun to remind myself that I am a quiet person by nature, socially adequate during most occasions, and often more quiet and reserved than others. I feel OK about this now, and realize that being reserved or outgoing is more in my control, that I act that way as I choose to, and that being reserved is acceptable. When I take responsibility for that behavior, and don't attribute it to a basic personality inadequacy, I can accept my quietness much more. I realize and accept now that I need not be outgoing and talkative at all times. I also accept in me the times when I choose to pull back and build up strength and resources for being more outgoing at other times. However, I still don't **always** accept that, and can still feel inadequate sometimes for being reserved.

Besides paying closer attention to my patterns, being more self-aware, and self-accepting, I find that trying to avoid unwarranted assumptions and irrational beliefs is a help to me. Sometimes when I am quiet and others around me are actively conversing and enjoying each other's company, I begin to think that I am not liked. I think this stems from my early experiences when my mother paid such constant attention to me that I began to expect it from everyone. I later learned that I must give of myself to receive in return. But sometimes when I am not giving and am withdrawn, I begin to make the unwarranted assumption that others are rejecting me. When I think logically about this assumption and review my relationships with those I think are rejecting me, I realize that this is an irrational assumption. Then I can feel better about myself.

By and large, the constant care and concern to distinguish between irrational, baseless assumptions and facts about myself is a constant corrective to feelings of low self-esteem.

When I find myself tired, feeling low and unsuccessful in a particular venture, I remind myself that there is no rule that I must be perfect and successful in all things.

Another source of raising my self-esteem is **bibliotherapy**. Reading books about self-esteem, like the works of Albert Ellis, Carl Rogers, Abraham Maslow, Viktor Frankl, and others, I find that acknowledging the importance of self-esteem in a healthy personality helps me pay close attention to my own self-esteem and helps my rid myself of baseless ideas and assumptions which might tend to lower my self-esteem.

Studying the works of great thinkers in my religious heritage and in humanistic psychology helps me envision all human beings, including myself, as worthwhile, adequate, wholesome, unique creatures. Reading these ideas alone does not serve to completely remove feelings of inadequacy, but it serves as a catalyst and guide to find ways to raise my self-esteem.

In examining my own self-esteem I have found that I have both a generalized sense of self-esteem and specific notions about myself which can be high or low. My generalized feeling of self-esteem has always been high enough for me to resort to a gut-level feeling of OK-ness, which enabled me to lift myself by my bootstraps, when feeling low and inadequate. I have always had a deep, unshakable belief that I am a growing person, becoming more mature, more fully human, and more competent and adequate in every way, as the years go by. This overall sense of OK-ness has been one of the most significant factors in helping me seek ways to raise my particularized aspects of low self-esteem.

I find that my self-esteem often rises and falls, within a moderate range, and that finding ways to raise it is of great help. When I read Carl Rogers' phrase, "trusting one's organism"[2] I resonate deeply and intensely. More and more in the past several years I have learned to trust my own organism. I have learned to check inside myself, to my "listening eye," to use Bugenthal's phrase.[3] When I can trust myself and be myself, as I would like to be, I feel good, adequate, worthwhile, and content. Much of this has come about through academic training in humanistic psychology, intensive growth experiences in growth centers and human potential training events, as well as in personal psychotherapy.

Because I have grown so much in intensive group experiences, I believe in this approach very deeply. Had I not witnessed the growth I have achieved in my own case, I could not commit myself the way I am to the Human Potential Movement. I have found, furthermore, that the progress I have made in improving my self-image and raising my self-esteem have been the most significant factors in my personal growth. It is for this reason that I believe so deeply in the potential of the self-esteem laboratory.

FOOTNOTES

1. Cf., among others, Erving and Miriam Polster, **Gestalt Therapy Integrated** (New York: Vintage Books, 1973), especially pp. 207-232. See also James F. T. Bugental, **The Search for Authenticity** (New York: Holt, Rinehart and Winston, 1965), chapter 13, "Awareness: The Basic Process of Being," pp. 217-234.

2. **On Becoming a Person** (Boston: Houghton Mifflin, 1961), pp. 175, 189-191, and many other passages.

3. James F. T. Bugental, "The Listening Eye," **Journal of Humanistic Psychology,** Volume 16, Number 1, 1976, pp. 55-66.

FOR FURTHER READING

Gerard Egan, **Face to Face—The Small Group Experience and Interpersonal Growth.** Chapter 5, "Self-Disclosure," pp. 40-60. Monterey, Ca.: Brooks/Cole, 1973.

Sidney M. Jourard, **Disclosing Man to Himself.** New York: Van Nostrand Reinhold, 1968.

_____ , **The Transparent Self.** New York: Van Nostrand, 1971.

Ira Progroff, **At a Journal Workshop.** New York: Dialogue House Library, 1975.

Chapter 5

DESIGNS FOR SELF-ESTEEM LABS

General Considerations

In creating the proper design for a particular client group, it is important for the facilitator to keep several questions in mind. [1]

1) What are the goals of this particular lab? Effective laboratory education should be goal-oriented to avoid the problems and pitfalls of the over-generalized "wow effect," namely, that persons enjoy being close to others and sharing their lives together in an intensive workshop experience but do not come away with any specific behavioral changes and pointed achievements in personal and/or professional growth. Such carefully defined goals not only help the facilitator achieve the desired effects geared for the group at hand, but they also act as motivators for participants during the training experiences.

2) What are the special sensitivities, background, and prior experience of the present group? This information will help the facilitator make the choices between different kinds of structured experiences, from the least threatening to the most potentially unsettling, from heavily experiential to heavily cognitive. Clarity as to probable participant responses will help assure the success of the design components selected.

3) What **sequence** is being followed? Are the combinations of small groups, lecturettes, structured experiences and instrumentation carefully modulated and sequenced to provide maximum involvement, continuity and cumulative impact?

4) Is there enough choice to assure on-the-spot **flexibility?** Is the lab sufficiently "overdesigned" to assure several options at any given point, depending on the group climate, level of interest, atmosphere of trust? Is ample opportunity built into the design to receive feedback from the group as to its needs and interests at periodic checkpoints during the training event?

6) Is there adequate time built into the design for processing? Is enough time allowed for participants to evaluate and integrate the data generated by the design? If the lab experience is to be maximally effective in terms of back-home transfer and application of attitudes, values, skills and new behavior, there must be sufficient opportunity to talk through the behavioral and feeling data that emerge. It is precisely because many human relations training events do not allow sufficient time for processing, that harmful experiences occasionally occur. Intensive emotional experiences must be sufficiently worked through prior to departure. Otherwise it is possible that hanging data might be integrated in dysfunctional ways. Perhaps the key to the success of the entire lab experience hinges on sufficient and effective processing of experience-based learnings.

Design Components

Included in the several suggested designs below are various laboratory components, including small group meetings, structured experiences, lecturettes and instruments. Each proposed design has a careful balance of these different components.

1) Small groups

    Processing of structured experiences, as indicated above, is a vital and indispensable ingredient in laboratory learning. This processing frequently takes place in small groups which convene following structured experiences. The conventional use of small groups in laboratory learning, such as T-groups or growth groups, is not included in these self-esteem lab designs since this lab is specifically geared for skill training through more structured formats.

2) Structured experiences

    Use, principles and details of suggested structured experiences for the self-esteem lab are included in Chapter 6 of this **Handbook.**

3) Lecturettes

    Sources for lecturettes include material in this Handbook such as Chapter 2 on definitions and components of self-esteem, Chapter 3 on the affirmation model, and Chapter 7 on self-esteem for minority groups. The bibliography provides ample resources for further study and reading on the subject of self-esteem.

Appended to the suggested designs included in this chapter are brief readings which can be used effectively within lecturettes on general themes or as the basis of a specific lecturette itself. Other similar readings which can be used to supplement lecturettes can be found in the writer's collection, **Glad to Be Me** (Prentice-Hall, 1976).

In addition to these readings several audio-visual aids are available for introductions to lecturettes, summaries, or major content material:

a) Sidney B. Simon's delightful booklet called IALAC (I Am Loveable and Capable), available in bulk for 50c each from Argus Communications, 7440 Natchez Avenue, Niles, Ill. 60648. Also available from Argus is a cassette or record and filmstrip of the IALAC story ($20) for filmstrip and record or cassette). IALAC can be used with special effect with parents, teachers and other helping agents.

b) A brief 3-minute film entitled "Claude" talks about a little boy whose parents constantly put him down, saying "Claude, you'll never amount to anything." Claude surprises them and becomes an ingenious inventor. See Chapter 8 on curricular materials for rental or purchase details.

c) Several cassette lectures are available for use by participants between sessions, or segments of the tapes during sessions, by Nathaniel Branden, author of **The Psychology of Self-Esteem.** These are available from Audio-Forum, 422 First Street, S.E., Washington, D.C. 20003. One is called "Basic Relaxation and Ego-Strengthening Program," 25 minutes, Tape 599, $10 purchase price. Another is "Self-Esteem," 75 minutes, Tape 567, $8.95. Another cassette tape is available from **Libertarian Review,** 410 First Street S.E., Washington, D.C. 20003, entitled "Nathaniel Branden Discusses Self-Esteem," 88 minutes, Tape 802, $13.50. A free catalog of other resources is available from both organizations listing offerings by Branden and others on related themes. Several cassette-type lectures on self-esteem by the author of this book are available by writing the publisher of this book, Growth Associates.

4) Instrumentation

Paper and pencil instruments which measure self-concept can be used both to assess the level of success of a self-esteem laboratory, and to evaluate the level of self-esteem in a client in psychotherapy, or a student in an experiential workshop.

It will be helpful, therefore, to survey some of the problems in self concept measurement and some of the more frequently utilized instruments.

Combs, Avila and Purkey distinguish between self concept and self-report.[2] The most obvious way to determine the contours of one's self concept would seem to be to ask the person involved. However, it is not as easy as it sounds, say these authors. Since one's self-perception is a private matter, the person may not be willing to reveal to a scientific investigator what lies beneath his skin. Furthermore, even if the subject is willing, who is to say that his own subjective report is accurate? It is surely not an easy task for a person to describe himself and his self image. Thus, persons using the standard self concept instruments must beware not to confuse self concept with self-report. The former is what the subjects believes about himself, while the latter is "what a person is willing or able to divulge, or what he can be tricked into saying about himself...."[2]

Nevertheless, self-reports are valuable data for the researcher. A self-report is observable behavior, and as such it is "an expression of the subject's perceptual field at the moment of acting. Because of its symbolic character and the uses the behavior makes of it for self-expression, it has more than ordinary value for helping us understand another person."[3]

Despite its limitations, several prominent social scientists, such as Rogers and Allport,[4] accept self-reports as important sources of information about the individual. LaBenne and Greene, while agreeing that there are many difficulties in measuring self concept, nevertheless find existing instruments to be the best tools we have.[5]

Purkey gives a brief and useful review of self-report inventories currently available.[6] Three instruments listed by Gibb as being used mostly widely today in evaluating human relations training are: Shostrom's Personal Orientation Inventory, measuring self-actualization, William C. Schutz's FIRO Scale B (Behavior), and William Fitts' Tennessee Self Concept Scale.[7]

Shostrom's POI includes two variables of twelve which apply directly to our laboratory: self regard and self acceptance.[8] This instrument has wide acceptance in the field, is available commercially, and may be handscored or computer scored. Schutz's FIRO-B measures expressed and wanted inclusion, control, and affection.[9]

The Tennessee Self Concept Scale (TSCS), which measures the effects of the self-esteem lab most directly, was developed by William Fitts as the primary instrument in a research project on vocational rehabilitation. It has been standardized, and is now widely used in self concept research with a broad range of people. Fitts' hypothesis that "the self concept is an index of self-actualization or personality integration," has been supported in studies by him and others.[10]

Furthermore, the TSCS fits well with the criteria established by Pfeiffer and Heslin for an effective human relations instrument.[11] These criteria fall under the following headings: validity, reliability, objectivity, availability, cost, time, sophistication, complexity and supplementation.

The TSCS consists of 100 self-descriptive statements by which the subject draws his own picture of himself. It is a self administering instrument used with subjects age 12 or higher and having a reading level of at least sixth grade. It is applicable to the whole spectrum of psychological adjustment from healthy people to psychotic patients. The TSCS is completed generally in 10 to 20 minutes, with a mean time of about 13 minutes.

Of the 100 self-descriptive statements, to which the subject responds on a five-point response scale ranging from "completely true" to "completely false," ten come from the MMPI L-Scale and make up the Self Criticism Score, a measure of overt defensiveness. The other 90 items were selected from a large pool of self-descriptions of patients and non-patients. Seven clinical psychologists were chosen to judge and classify these items and the final 90 statements are those upon which there was perfect agreement by the judges.

The TSCS includes a scale of Positive Scores which represent a person's internal frame of reference, including Total Positive, Positive Identity, Positive Self Satisfaction, Positive Behavior, Positive Physical Self, Positive Moral-Ethical Self, Positive Personal Self, Positive Family Self and Positive Social Self.[12]

The Scale also includes six Empirical Scales derived from testing various groups often seen in a clinical setting. These scales are Defensive Positive, General Maladjustment, Psychosis, Personality Disorder, Neurosis, and Personality Integration. Further detailed explanation about the TSCS and various important implications derived from its field usage can be found in a series of seven excellent monographs produced by Fitts and his associates.[13]

DESIGN I: Weekend Lab

Friday Night
    Themes: 1) Community Building 2) Introduction to Concept of Self Esteem and Validation
    Structured Experience: Wheel-in-a-Wheel

Structured Experience: Being Inspired
Structured Experience: Centering
Lecturette: a) Introduction to Self-Esteem
            b) Validation/Affirmation/Stroking
Structured Experience: The Three V's
Structured Experience: Killer Statements
Structured Experience: Proud Whip
Instrument: Personal Orientation Inventory (POI), FIRO-B or Tennessee Self Concept Scale (TSCS)
Reading and/or Lecturette: "Please Hear What I Am Not Saying"
(**Glad to Be Me**)

Saturday Morning
Themes: 1) Self Acceptance 2) Self-Ideal Discrepancy
Structured Experience: Coat of Arms
Structured Experience: Three Unique Things
Lecturette: a) Real Self and Ideal Self
            b) The Importance of Self-Acceptance
Structured Experience: Childhood Visions of Myself
Structured Experience: Pooling Faults and Flaws
Structured Experience: Accepting our Weaknesses
Instrument: Nourishing-Toxic Living Scale
(**Glad To Be Me**)

Saturday Afternoon
Themes: 1) Self-Validation 2) Self-Esteem for Helpers
Structured Experience: Poem About Me
Structured Experience: Ad for Yourself or My Obituary
Lecturette: The Difference Between Selfishness and Self-Esteem
Structured Experience: Massage Train
Structured Experience: Car Wash
Reading and/or Lecturette: I.A.L.A.C.—Self-Esteem for Parents, Teachers, Clergy and Other Helpers
Structured Experience: How Perceptive You Are!
Structured Experience: Animal Farm
Film: Claude
Reading: "The Little Boy" by Helen E. Buckley
(**Glad To Be Me**)
Structured Experience: I Appreciate

Saturday Night
Themes: 1) Imagery 2) Body Image
Structured Experience: Thumb Wrestling
Structured Experience: Apple Image
Structured Experience: Power of Imagery
Lecturette: Imagery and Its Potential for Human Development
Structured Experience: Who Are You?
Structured Experience: Strength Bombardment
Structured Experience: Expanding Self Concept
Structured Experience: Proud Whip (Something about my body I'm proud of is...")

Structured Experience: Boast (Specifically related to the body)
Structured Experience: Group Applause
Structured Experience: Non-verbal Feedback
Reading and/or Lecturette: Virginia Satir's Declaration of Self-Esteem
(**Glad To Be Me**)

Sunday Morning

Themes: 1) Self-Awareness 2) Raising Self-Esteem 3) Closure
Structured Experience: Dr. Jekyll and Mr. Hyde
Structured Experience: Pick A Poster
Instrument: Self-Actualization Check List (Appended to this Chapter)
Structured Experience: Dual Personalities
Structured Experience: Wise Old Man Fantasy
Structured Experience: No Matter What You Say
Reading and/or Lecturette: Warm Fuzzies
Structured Experience: Cheerleader
Structured Experience: Body Lift
Instrument: Post-Test
Evaluation and Feedback
Structured Experience: Toast

DESIGN II: Week-Long for Counselors, Teachers, Clergy and Other Helping Professionals

Note: This design is divided into twelve sessions, as follows: Monday morning, afternoon, evening (3)
Tuesday morning, afternoon, evening (3)
Wednesday morning, afternoon (2)
(In most week-long training events, Wednesday night is the "night-off")
Thursday morning, afternoon, evening (3)
Friday morning (1)

The same design can be used for a twelve week course, holding one three-hour session per week.

Session #1

Theme: a) Community building
b) Introduction to Concept of Self-Esteem
c) Validation/Affirmation/Stroking
Structured Experience: Wheel-in-a-Wheel
Structured Experience: Being Inspired
Structured Experience: Centering
Lecturette a) Introduction to Concept of Self-Esteem
b) Validation/Affirmation/Stroking
Structured Experience: The Three V's
Structured Experience: Killer Statements
Structured Experience: Proud Whip
Reading and/or Lecturette("Please Hear What I Am Not Saying"
(**Glad To Be Me**)

Session #2
Theme: Real Self vs. Ideal Self
  Structured Experience: Coat of Arms
  Structured Experience: Childhood Visions of Myself
  Lecturette: The Real Self and the Ideal Self
  Structured Experience: First Impressions
  Structured Experience: Who Are You?
  Instrument: Shostrom's POI, Schutz's FIRO-B or Fitts' TSCS (Pre-test)
  Structured Experience: A Time To Throw Stones
  Reading and/or Lecturette: Maslow's Hierarchy of Needs (Appended to this Chapter)

Session #3
Theme: Self Acceptance
  Structured Experience: Proud Whip
  Structured Experience: Pooling Faults and Flaws
  Lecturette: Self Acceptance
  Structured Experience: Accepting our Weaknesses
  Structured Experience: Trusting Your Organism
  Instrument: Nourishing-Toxic Living Scale **(Glad To Be Me)**
  Structured Experience: Good What?
  Structured Experience: Poem About Me
  Reading and/or Lecturette: Fritz Perls' Gestalt Prayer (Appended to this Chapter)

Session #4
Theme: Self-Validation
  Structured Experience: Proud Whip ("Something I'm proud that I did at this workshop is...")
  Structured Experience: An Ad for Myself
  Structured Experience: My Obituary
  Lecturette: The Difference Between Selfishness and Self-Esteem
  Structured Experience: How Perceptive You Are!
  Structured Experience: Self-Esteem Tree
  Reading and/or Lecturette: Stanley Herman's poem, "Selfishness" **(Glad To Be Me)**
  Structured Experience: Massage Train
  Structured Experience: Three Unique Things

Session #5
Theme: Self-Esteem and Behavior
  Structured Experience: Expanding Self Concept
  Structured Experience: Dr. Jekyll and Mr. Hyde
  Lecturette: Self-Esteem and Its Influence on Behavior
  Structured Experience: Pick A Poster
  Lecturette/Discussion: Behavioral Model for Personal Growth (Appended to this Chapter)
  Structured Experience: Who Are You?
  Structured Experience: Thumb Wrestling
  Structured Experience: Car Wash

Session #6
  Theme: Group Validation
    Structured Experience: This Is Your Life
    Structured Experience: Epitaph
    Structured Experience: Cheerleader
    Structured Experience: Strength Bombardment
    Lecturette: a) Importance of Supportive Atmosphere for Personal Growth
              b) Back Home Support Groups
    Structured Experience: Massage Train
    Structured Experience: Body Lift
    Structured Experience: Caring Lift
    Reading and/or Lecturette: Warm Fuzzies
Session #7
  Theme: Imagery
    Structured Experience: Apple Image
    Structured Experience: Power of Imagery
    Structured Experience: The Image I Project
    Lecturette: The Magic Power of Imaging and Self-Imagery
    Structured Experience: Reaching for a High
    Structured Experience: Car Wash
    Structured Experience: Proud Whip ("I'm proud that I use my creative imagination when I...")
    Structured Experience: I Appreciate
Session #8
  Theme: Self-Awareness
    Structured Experience: Epitaph
    Structured Experience: Boast
    Structured Experience: Picture of Me (see Poem About Me)
    Instrument: Self-Actualization Check List (Appended)
    Structured Experience: Dual Personalities
    Structured Experience: Group Applause
    Reading and/or Lecturette: Satir's Declaration of Self-Esteem (**Glad To Be Me**)
    Structured Experience: I Appreciate
Session #9
  Theme: Raising Self-Esteem
    Structured Experience: Centering
    Structured Experience: Proud Whip
    Structured Experience: First Impressions (Re-check)
    Lecturette: Factors That Raise and Lower Self-Esteem
    Structured Experience: No Matter What You Say
    Structured Experience: Expanding Self Concept (repeat)
    Structured Experience: Wise Old Man Fantasy
    Reading and/or Lecturette: "The Little Boy" by Helen E. Buckley (**Glad To Be Me**)
    Structured Experience: Non-verbal Feedback

Session #10

Theme: Self-Esteem for Counselors, Teachers, Clergy, Parents, and Other Helpers

Structured Experience: Proud Whip ("I'm proud of something I did to raise the self-esteem of my clients, students, etc....")

Structured Experience: Nurturing Relationships

Structured Experience: Ad for Yourself (to get a job in your profession)

Lecturette: Ways to Build High Self-Esteem in Clients, Students, Children, etc.

Structured Experience: Massage Train

Structured Experience: Pick A Poster (With specific application to professional life)

Lecturette: Grading and Evaluation and their effects on subordinates

Structured Experience: Car Wash

Structured Experience: Group Applause

Lecturette/Discussion: IALAC (include Cassette and Filmstrip)

Structured Experience: I Appreciate

Session #11

Theme: Self Image and the Body

Structured Experience: A Drawing of Me (see Poem About Me)

Structured Experience: Proud Whip ("The part of my body I like the most is...")

Structured Experience: Accepting Our Weaknesses (Specifically related to body and body image)

Lecturette: Self-Esteem and Its Relation to Our Bodies

Structured Experience: Three Unique Things (About My Body)

Structured Experience: No Matter What You Say (About My Body)

Structured Experience: Body Lift

Structured Experience: Caring Lift

Structured Experience: Car Wash (especially validating body)

Structured Experience: Pooling Faults and Flaws (Related to body)

Structured Experience: Non-verbal feedback

Structured Experience: I Appreciate

Session #12

Theme: a) Minority Groups and Their Self Concept
       b) Closure

Structured Experience: Proud Whip ("I'm proud I am black, Jewish, etc., because ..."—or "I'm proud of my relationship with Jews, blacks, etc., because...")

Structured Experience: Expanding Self Concept (Relating to Minority Groups)

Structured Experience: Three Unique Things (About me, others, re minority group status)

Lecturette: Minority Group Members and Their Self Concept. Ways to raise my self concept as a minority group member. Ways to raise the self concept of my clients, students, etc., who are minority group members

Structured Experience: Nurturing Relationships (Related to Minority Groups)
Structured Experience: Killer Statements (Related to Minority Groups)
Structured Experience: Coat of Arms (Related to Minority Groups)
Structured Experience: Ad for My Group (see Ad for Yourself)
Structured Experience: No Matter What You Say (Related to Minority Group Killer Statements)
Structured Experience: Massage Train
Lecturette: Validation and disvalidation and their effects. Film: Claude
Instrument: FIRO-B, POI or TSCS (Post-test)
Evaluation and Feedback
Structured Experience: Toast

A SELF-ACTUALIZATION CHECK LIST

I am in the process of becoming a more Self-actualized person by:

		Yes	?	No
Understanding basic human needs	1. Caring for my own basic physical needs such as food, shelter, clothing, and good health			
	2. Loving my self and others			
	3. Risking, creating, exploring			
	4. Learning, studying, and thinking			
	5. Helping and working with others			
	6. Accepting my strengths and limitations			
	7. Striving for dignity and self respect			
Expressing human feeling	8. Being open and spontaneous			
	9. Expressing joy and happiness through laughter, smiles, and cheer			
	10. Becoming close, intimate, and loving with another person			
	11. Expressing grief and sadness with tears and anguish			
	12. Expressing my fears, anxieties and worries			
	13. Expressing the anger and frustration in my life			
	14. Celebrating life with others			
Self-awareness and control	15. Becoming aware of my body sensations of breathing, seeing, hearing, tasting, touching, and smelling			
	16. Having faith in my unique talents and abilities			
	17. Becoming aware of and sensitive to the feelings of others			
	18. Inhibiting and controlling my undesirable behaviors			
	19. Planning and directing my own future			

		Yes	?	No
Becoming aware of human values	20. Rewarding and reinforcing my desirable behaviors			
	21. Wishing, fantasizing, and daydreams			
	22. Practicing social skills of courtesy, honesty, and cooperation			
	23. Developing an awareness of the importance of knowledge, power, and wealth			
	24. Nurturing, serving, and nourishing others			
	25. Developing awareness and appreciation of beauty, art, and music			
	26. Committing myself to selected values and expectations			
	27. Learning to love and care more fully			
Developing social and personal maturity	28. Anticipating the consequences of my own behavior			
	29. Assuming self-determination and responsibility			
	30. Adapting to personal, social, and technological change			
	31. Assuming community and social responsibility			
	32. Altruistically identifying with and aiding others			
	33. Transcending myself through universal identification			
	34. Renewing and re-creating my Self			

Additional Comments:

Source:
Robert Valett, **Self-Actualization** (Niles, Ill.: Argus Communications, 1974), page 95.

ABRAHAM MASLOW'S HIERARCHY OF NEEDS

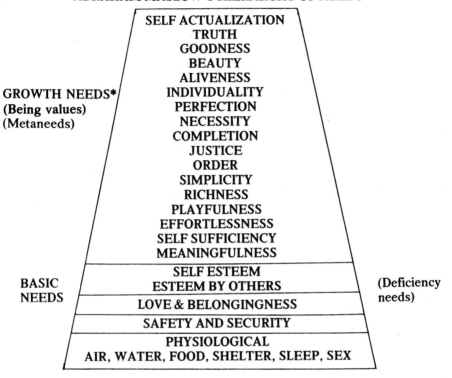

GROWTH NEEDS*
(Being values)
(Metaneeds)

SELF ACTUALIZATION
TRUTH
GOODNESS
BEAUTY
ALIVENESS
INDIVIDUALITY
PERFECTION
NECESSITY
COMPLETION
JUSTICE
ORDER
SIMPLICITY
RICHNESS
PLAYFULNESS
EFFORTLESSNESS
SELF SUFFICIENCY
MEANINGFULNESS

**BASIC
NEEDS**

SELF ESTEEM
ESTEEM BY OTHERS
LOVE & BELONGINGNESS
SAFETY AND SECURITY
PHYSIOLOGICAL
AIR, WATER, FOOD, SHELTER, SLEEP, SEX

(Deficiency
needs)

THE EXTERNAL ENVIRONMENT
PRECONDITIONS FOR NEED SATISFACTION
FREEDOM, JUSTICE, ORDERLINESS

CHALLENGE (STIMULATION)

*Growth needs are all of equal importance (not hierarchical)

Source:
Frank C. Gobel, **The Third Force** (New York: Pocket Books, 1971), p. 52.

Fritz Perls' **Gestalt Prayer**

I do my thing, and you do your thing.
I am not in this world to live up to your expectations
And you are not in this world to live up to mine.
You are you and I am I,
And if by chance we find each other, it's beautiful.
If not, it can't be helped.

* * *

A Behavioral Model for Personal Growth

Dr. Carl Rogers, in his 1961 book **On Becoming a Person,** has identified three characteristics of personal growth. These lend themselves to use as models in the process of developing personal growth. The checklist has been developed by Dr. Robert E. Alberti, based upon Rogerian phrases:

"An Increasing Openness to Experience"

How recently have you

- participated in a new sport or game?
- changed your views on an important (political, personal, professional) issue?
- tried a new hobby or craft?
- studied a new language or culture?
- spend fifteen minutes or more paying attention to your body feelings, senses (relaxation, tension, sensuality)?
- listened for fifteen minutes or more to a religious, political, professional, or personal viewpoint with which you disagreed?
- tasted a new food, smelled a new odor, listened to a new sound?
- allowed yourself to cry? or to say "I care about you"? or to laugh until you cried? or to scream at the top of your lung capacity? or to admit you were afraid?
- watched the sun (or moon) rise or set? or a bird soar on the wind's currents? or a flower open to the sun?
- traveled to a place you had never been before?
- made a new friend? or cultivated an old friendship?
- spent an hour or more really communicating (actively listening and responding honestly) with a person of a different cultural or racial background?
- taken a "fantasy trip"—allowing your imagination to run freely for ten minutes to an hour or more?

"Increasingly Existential Living"

How recently have you

- done something you felt like doing at that moment, without regard for the consequences?
- stopped to "listen" to what was going on inside you?
- spontaneously expressed a feeling—anger, joy, fear, sadness, caring —without "thinking about it"?
- done what you wanted to do, instead of what you thought you "should" do?
- allowed yourself to spend time or money on an immediate "payoff" rather than saving for tomorrow?
- bought something you wanted "on impulse"?
- done something no one (including you) expected you to do?

"An Increasing Trust in One's Organism"

How recently have you

- done what felt right to you, against the advice of others?
- allowed yourself to experiment creatively with new approaches to old problems?

- expressed an unpopular opinion assertively in the face of majority opposition
- used your own intellectual reasoning ability to work out a solution to a difficult problem?
- made a decision and acted upon it right away?
- acknowledged by your actions that you can direct your own life?
- cared enough about yourself to get a physical exam (within a year)?
- told others of your religious faith, or philosophy of life?
- assumed a position of leadership in your profession, or an organization, or your community?
- asserted your feelings when you were treated unfairly?
- risked sharing your personal feelings with another person?
- designed and/or built something on your own?
- admitted you were wrong?

Source:

Your Perfect Right (2nd ed.) by Robert E. Alberti and Michael L. Emmons (San Luis Obispo, Ca.: Impact Publishers, 1970).

FOOTNOTES

1. J. William Pfeiffer and John E. Jones, "Design considerations in Laboratory Education," **The 1973 Annual Handbook for Group Facilitators** (La Jolla, Ca.: University Associates, 1973), pp. 177-194.
2. **Helping Relationships** (Boston: Allyn and Bacon 1971), p. 52.
3. **Ibid.**, p. 54.
4. William W. Purkey, **Self Concept and School Achievement** (Englewood Cliffs, N.J.: Prentice-Hall, 1970), p. 59.
5. **Educational Implications of Self-Concept Theory** (Pacific Palisades, Ca.: Goodyear, 1969), pp. 117-118.
6. **Op. cit.** (note 4), pp. 61-2.
7. Jack R. Gibb, "The Message from Research," in John Jones and J. William Pfeiffer (eds.), **The 1974 Annual Handbook for Group Facilitators** (La Jolla, Ca.: University Associates, 1974), p. 156.
8. **Personal Orientation Inventory Manual** (San Diego: Educational and Industrial Testing Service, 1974).
9. **The FIRO Scales Manual** (Palo Alto: Consulting Psychologists Press, 1967), p. 8.
10. William H. Fitts, **The Self Concept and Self-Actualization** (Nashville, Tenn.: Counselor Recordings and Tests, 1971), p. 71.
11. **Instrumentation in Human Relations Training** (La Jolla, Ca.: University Associates, 1973), p. 27.
12. Fitts, **Op. cit.**, pp. 41-45.
13. The entire series of seven monographs is available from Counselor Recordings and Tests, Box 6184, Acklen Station, Nashville, Tenn. 37212, for $18. The Scale is available in a new computer form along with a scoring system for quantity scoring. The computer output provides a profile of 29 variables, group means and standard deviations for each variable, and punched IBM output for further statistical work. The regular form of the Scale, still available, may be hand- or computer-scored. Test booklets (computer form) are $.20 each, or $.18 each for 100 or more. The Manual is $.90, and computer processing is $.55 each for fifty or more.

FURTHER READING ON INSTRUMENTATION

A.W. Combs, D.W. Soper, and C.C. Courson. "The Measurement of Self-Concept and Self-Report," **Educational and Psychological Measurement,** 23 (1963), 493-500.

William H. Fitts. **Manual for the Tennessee Self Concept Scale.** Nashville: Counselor Recordings and Tests, 1965.

_____ . **The Self Concept and Self-Actualization.** Nashville: Counselor Recordings and Tests, 1971.

Jack R. Gibb. "The Message from Research," in J. Jones and W. Pfeiffer (eds.), **The 1974 Annual Handbook for Group Facilitators** La Jolla, Ca.: University Associates, 1974, pp. 155-177.

Wallace D. LaBenne and Bert I. Greene. **Educational Implications of Self-Concept Theory,** Pacific Palisades, Ca.: Goodyear, 1969, Chapter 9, "The Measurement of Self-Concept," pp. 109-119.

J. William Pfeiffer and Richard Heslin. **Instrumentation in Human Relations Training.** La Jolla, Ca.: University Associates, 1973.

William W. Purkey. **Self Concept and School Achievement.** Englewood Cliffs, N.J.: Prentice-Hall, 1970. Cf. esp. pp. 58-65, "Problems in Evaluating the Self."

William C. Schutz. **The FIRO Scales Manual.** Palo Alto, Ca.: Consulting Psychologists Press, Inc., 1967.

Everett L. Shostrom. **Personal Orientation Inventory—Manual.** San Diego, Ca.: Educational and Industrial Testing Service, 1974.

Ruth C. Wiley. **The Self Concept: A Critical Survey of Pertinent Research Literature.** Lincoln, Neb.: University of Nebraska Press, 1961.

Chapter 6

STRUCTURED EXPERIENCES

Introduction

The structured experiences are the heart of the self-esteem laboratory. It is crucial, therefore, that they be used properly. It often appears that anyone may conduct an experiential education program, since no formal lecture is involved and learning emerges from the participation of the group. This is definitely not so, however. Unless adequately trained facilitators utilize these structured experiences, in all probability only a small part of their potential effects will be realized. In such a case these experiences become more sophisticated parlor games than meaningful educational activities. The structured experiences are basically means to an end, not ends in themselves, i.e., not just "fun and games." Particularly when dealing with a delicate theme such as one's self-esteem, the possibility for deep feelings being activited is likely. Led by an untrained person, the danger of inadequate handling of a deeply emotional situation escalates.

Effective facilitators of experiential education should be persons who radiate confidence, have a disciplined approach to goal-setting and directionality in realizing the goals, sensitivity and warmth to create a supportive atmosphere, and an enthusiastic approach to laboratory education. They should be persons with adequate administrative skills to enable the group to move forward in a well-ordered fashion and create confidence in them as trustworthy authorities, and should be effective discussion leaders since much of the ultimate learning flows out of the reflective dialog and group discussion following the structured experiences. Self-esteem lab facilitators should be versed in group dynamics, pedagogy, child and family development, and human relations training.

The following five steps should be utilized in carrying out an experiential learning model:

1) **Experiencing**
   The structured experience is carried out with the guidance of the facilitator

2) **Publishing**
   Patricipants "publish" (report or share) their reactions and observations with others who have participated together with them or observed them

3) **Processing**
   After sharing reactions and observations, the dynamics that emerged from the experience are explored, discussed and evaluated (processed)

4) **Generalizing**
   This involves extracting general principles from the experience, or a statement of learnings which help define and clarify the experience

5) **Applying**
Once general principles are derived, it is crucial that some attempt be made to apply them to the lives of the participants.

STRUCTURED EXPERIENCES

WHEEL-IN-A-WHEEL: A Self-Esteem Warm-Up
Goals
    I. A warm-up exercise for community building
    II. To set the stage for self- and other-affirmation
    III. Experiencing self-disclosure as a way of building self-esteem and self-acceptance
Group Size
    At least fourteen people
Time Required
    Thirty minutes
Materials
    No special material required
Physical Setting
    Two concentric circles of chairs, the same number in each circle, with each chair in the inner circle facing a chair in the outer circle, so that a dyadic arrangement is made. For example, with 16 chairs, 8 in the outer circle, and 8 in the inner circle, and one person in the inner circle facing one in the outer, there would be eight dyads. Each dyad is composed of one person in the outer circle and one person in the inner circle.
Process
    I. Facilitator asks the group to be seated in the two concentric circles, with each person having a partner in the other circle. He gives them a topic to discuss, giving them each one minute to discuss it, and then the other partner has one minute on the same topic.
    II. After that two minute discussion, each person in the inner circle moves one seat to the left and has a new partner. The new dyad then discusses question number two, and so on, until all of the allotted questions have been answered.
Variations
    I. To permit those in the same circle to get to know each other, an additional activity can be added. Each circle group goes to a different end of the room. If there are eight in each circle, for example, then in each end of the room there are two rows of four chairs each facing each other. The same procedure as before is followed, with each dyadic partner dealing with an issue, and then each person on one of the rows moving to the left, with the person on the end going to the extreme right chair. Then the next question is asked, etc., until all the people in one row have spoken to the others in the opposite row. New questions should be used in these dyadic discussions, not the ones discussed in the circles.

SUGGESTED DISCUSSION QUESTIONS FOR WHEEL-IN-A-WHEEL
(Note: Questions should move from the less threatening to the more intimate)
1. Talk about a place you like to be.
2. A recent vacation you enjoyed.
3. Something you do well.

4. Something you fixed or repaired.
5. Nice things people have said about you.
6. An award you received, or would like to receive.
7. What do you do when you get angry?
8. How do you take criticism?
9. Think of a time you felt very good about yourself.
10. Think of a time you felt very bad about yourself.
11. Something creative you did recently.
12. Something compassionate you did recently.
13. Someone whose life you influenced.
14. How do you feel about yourself?
15. A peak experience you had.
16. Some place where you feel totally accepted.

References

Nancy Geyer and Shirley Noll, **Team Building in Church Groups Team Building Services.** Service Dept., Board of Education, P.O. Box 871, Nashville, Tenn. 37202.

Brendon Reddy & Otto Kroeger, "Intergroup Model Building: The Lego Man," in **The 1972 Annual Handbook for Group Facilitators.**

BEING INSPIRED: Breathing for High Self-Esteem
Goals
    I. Convey idea that breathing is related to self concept and can have important effects on feelings about self and behavior.
    II. Practice deep-breathing exercises.
Group Size
Individual or group any size
Time Required
Five to ten minutes initially. Perhaps more time later if participants wish to itensify breathing training.
Materials
No special materials required
Physical Setting
Room for each participant to have enough space to feel free and relaxed
Process
    I. Facilitator explains that the word "inspiration" means taking in air, or spirit, inhaling, breathing. Often people who are afraid or emotionally tense hold their breath and cut off painful feellings. Over a period of time we become accustomed to shallow breathing and become tense and physically restricted, constrained and "up-tight." A person with a poor self concept will often feel that he has low energy and power, emotionally and physically. Others may associate inhaling with taking in their fair share of life and the world. One whose self-image is that of a greedy person or undeserving will not be able to breathe deeply and take in life-giving oxygen. Others may be shy and by holding their breath and tightening their muscles may be unconsciously be playing dead and hope that others will not observe them. Thus, correct breathing is important to establish high self-esteem.
    II. Each person relaxes, sits up comfortably and takes a deep breath, filling entire chest cavity, lungs and stomach with air. Exhale. Repeat several times. This should help a person "center" inside himself and relax.
    III. Repeat, and focus on nothing but your own breathing. This takes the mind off of other anxieties, bemoaning the past or worrying about the future. Focusing on breathing keeps one in the here-and-now, where anxiety is usually absent. (Most anxiety comes from living in the past or future).
    IV. Group may wish to discuss new feeling of relaxation and what it does for their self-esteem. Describe feelings of self-esteem in detail.
    V. This deep breathing should be repeated frequently during a group's life to achieve relaxation and high self-esteem.

DR. JEKYLL AND MR. HYDE: Our Many Selves

Goals
  I. To build self-awareness through recognizing our many different personalities.
  II. To recognize the complex nature of our personality and behavior patterns.

Group Size
Unlimited groups of four to six

Time Required
One hour

Materials
Several copies of the Situation-Feelings-Behavior Sheet for each person

Physical Setting
Place for individuals to write and small groups of four to six to have discussion

Process
  I. Facilitator explains that each person has many different personalities, moods, levels of excitement or boredom, depending on the circumstances, the company, and the context. It is helpful to be in touch with and accept all these different parts of ourselves to be totally self-accepting.
  II. Each person will have approximately thirty minutes to fill out the S-F-B Sheet (Situation-Feeling-Behavior Sheet). Think of several different contrasting situations in which your feelings and behaviors differ sharply. These are all part of you and should be "owned" by you, accepted by you as legitimate parts of yourself. List the situations in which such contrasting feelings and behaviors occur, and what specific feelings and behaviors you manifest at these differing times. For example, you may have one personality trying to get dressed and ready to leave in the morning for work, another having dinner in a romantic restaurant with your spouse or companion, another at work, another at a cocktail party, another watching a football game, another at a concert, another self having sexual relations. Be as specific and concrete as you can in describing the feelings and behaviors in each situation.
  III. Discuss in groups of four.
  IV. Facilitator leads discussion about learnings and applications emerging from this exercise.

Variation
  I. Role-playing one's various personalities may be appropriate for certain persons. A volunteer can select two or three contrasting situations in which he thinks, feels, behaves very differently, select persons from the group who most resemble the other persons in these situations, and act out the different ways he behaves in these circumstances.

This exercise was suggested by John E. Jones.

S-F-B Sheet

Describe three or four different situations or circumstances in which you may think, feel and act differently—several kinds of selves that you manifest in different circumstances, such as your family self, your public self, your working self. Then describe in detail the feelings and behaviors that accompany these differing selves.

SITUATION	FEELINGS	BEHAVIOR

ANIMAL FARM

Goals
    I. To build self-awareness
    II. To encourage re-owning of various emotional parts of participants.
    III. To draw upon the deeper levels of consciousness to sharpen our self-image and self-ideal.

Group Size
    Unlimited number of small groups of four to six

Time Required
    45 to 60 minutes

Materials
    None

Physical Setting
    Room for all the small groups to sit and talk

Process
    I. Facilitator asks each participant, to think of an animal they would like to be if they were to be an animal in the "next life."
    II. Take five minutes for each person to think, using his imagination, with eyes closed.
    III. Each person is then asked to discuss some or all of these questions:
        a) What I like about the animal
        b) What I don't like about that animal
        c) How I am like that animal
        d) How I'd like to more like that animal
        e) How I'd like to be less like that animal
    IV. Each person is then invited to talk about what he learned from the exercise, and what things he hopes to apply to his behavior and attitudes.

Variation
    I. Instead of an animal, the group may be asked to think of themselves as a tree, or a flower, and repeat the same process of which kind of flower, tree, they selected and why.
    II. Volunteers may be asked to nonverbally act like the animal, and then perhaps add some noises fitting in with their behavior. In the case of a tree or flower, the participants can sculpture themselves to be like a tree, flower, including facial expressions, body posture, etc.

I learned this exercise from Elaine Elkins

THIS IS YOUR LIFE: A Trip to Hollywood
Goals
   I. To enable participants to summarize their lives and get a broad perspective on their past, present and future.
  II. To help participants get in touch with their life goals, directions and objectives.
 III. To provide an opportunity for participants in a self-esteem lab to get to know each other through sharing a brief summary of their essential self and self-image.
Group Size
Ten or more
Time Required
Approximately thirty minutes
Materials
None
Physical Setting
No special requirements
Process
  I. Facilitator explains that Hollywood wants to do a movie of your life. Spend a few minutes quiet time thinking of a theme for the movie. (Pause for 3 minutes.) Now think for a title for the movie. (Pause for one minute).
 II. Form groups of 5 or 6 and share the theme and title of your life movie.

PICK A POSTER
Goals
I. To raise awareness of individual problems regarding self-esteem
II. To use group clusters as a way to share common problems in the area of self-esteem
Group Size
Best done with groups of twenty or more
Time Required
Thirty to forty-five minutes
Materials
Self-esteem posters, tape or thumb tacks
Physical Setting
A room with walls on which posters can be taped or tacked, and space near the walls for several small groups to gather
Process
I. Self-esteem posters are taped or tacked at various locations on the wall, spread out throughout the room. The facilitator reads the various posters and explains that these are words of advice regarding some of the main issues people deal with in regard to their self-esteem. At a given signal each person is to get up and move to the poster with which he most identifies, or which speaks to his own needs most directly.
II. After participants have joined in clusters near the poster they have selected, they may sit down and share why they chose this poster.
III. A few volunteers may share with the entire group some of the highlights of their group discussion, common themes, etc.
IV. Volunteers may make "I learned....", or "I rediscovered...." statements.
Variation
I. An interesting group activity, should there be time, during or prior to the workshop, would be to have a session in which the self-esteem posters are made. Participants can select from a number of sayings on a pre-distributed mimeographed sheet, or may make up their own, or find a saying or quotation from a book that is meaningful to them.
II. In the mailing about details regarding the self-esteem lab, participants may be invited or requested to bring one homemade self-esteem poster. This has the added effect of increasing involvement and anticipation before the beginning of the workshop.
III. If commercial posters are used, a contest of some sort can be used to determine who may take home a poster at the end of the workshop. A number of excellent posters on many different themes, including several relating to self-esteem, can be purchased from Argus Communications. These posters are exquisitely produced.
Possible Themes for Self-Esteem Posters
Lord, grant me a high opinion of myself. Prayer of an old Edinburgh weaver.

A man's interest in the world is only the overflow of his interest in himself. George Bernard Shaw.

Love of others and love of ourselves are not alternatives. On the contrary, an attitude of love towards themselves will be found in those who are capable of loving others. Erich Fromm.

As you love yourself, so shall you love others. Strange, but true, but with no exceptions. Harry Stack Sullivan.

If I am not for myself, who will be? Hillel.

God doesn't make junk. Marriage Encounter.

Self-trust is the first secret of success. Ralph Waldo Emerson.

No one can make you feel inferior without your consent. Eleanor Roosevelt.

Who can say more than this rich praise, that you alone are you? William Shakespeare.

No psychological health is possible unless this essential core of the person is fundamentally accepted, loved and respected by others and by himself...Abraham H. Maslow.

To be nobody—but myself—in a world that is doing its best, night and day, to make you everybody else—means to fight the hardest battle which any human being can fight, and never stop fighting. e. e. cummings.

So much is a man worth as he esteems himself. Francois Rabelais.

Oft times nothing profits more than self-esteem, grounded on just and right. John Milton.

Nothing is a greater impediment to being on good terms with others than being ill at ease with yourself. Honore de Balzac.

It's more important to be human than to be important. Anonymous.

If you can keep your head while all about you are losing theirs and blaming it on you, if you can trust yourself when all men doubt you... then you'll be a man, my son. Rudyard Kipling.

As soon as you trust yourself, you will know how to live. Goethe.

It's important to like yourself because wherever you go, you are going to take yourself along with you. Sidney Greenberg.

EPITAPH

Goals

I. To help participants take a long-range perspective on their life.

II. To encourage participants to summarize their life goals and achievements in a concise and succinct way.

III. To enable participants to establish closer contact with their own strengths and contributions to their families, professions and/or communities.

Group Size

Fifteen or more

Time Required

Forty-five minutes

Materials

Pencil or pen and paper

Physical Setting

A place to write

Process

I. Facilitator explains what an epitaph is—namely, a brief description of a person's life etched on the stone marker erected by one's grave. Those who have been to a cemetary might have seen one saying: Here lies William Fish, lover of humanity. Or: Manual Swerdlow, who raised the level of health care in his beloved community.

II. Facilitator invites each person to write a brief epitaph for his own life. It should be preferably under 25 words. The facilitator should suggest one he might write for his own life. Here is mine:

DOV ELKINS
Searcher for a fuller, richer, more meaningful
and exciting way of life for himself and others.

Variation

I. Participants can use paint or thick magic markers and draw their epitaph on construction paper cut in the shape of a tombstone, and then have them displayed on the walls or bulletin board.

II. This can be done at the beginning of a workshop and then again at end of the workshop, and see if any of them have changed.

Adapted from Simon, Howe and Kirschenbaum, **Values Clarification** (N.Y.: Hart, 1972), pp. 308-310.

II. Self Acceptance
  Pooling Faults and Flaws
  Good What?
  Accepting Our Weakness
  Trusting Our Organism

POOLING FAULTS AND FLAWS
Goals
   I. To promote self-acceptance through recognition that everyone has many faults and flaws
  II. To promote self-disclosure and openness in the group
 III. To promote a sense of community and group feeling
Group Size
Fifteen or more
Time Required
Thirty minutes
Materials
One 3x5 card and pencil for each group member
Physical Setting
Comfortable space to do writing and group role-playing
Process
   I. Facilitator distributes one 3x5 card and pencil, both of which are uniform for entire group. Facilitator explains that each person will write on the card in block printing a list of three of his most serious faults or flaws, inadequacies or shortcomings. Facilitator explains that this will be done anonymously, hence the block printing and uniform cards and pencils.
  II. Facilitator collects cards face down first from men and shuffles them thoroughly. He then redistributes them at random to the men. He then repeats for women.
 III. Each member then reads off the card the faults listed, as if they were his own, and role plays them. Participant should explain and amplify the faults, pointing out the problems they cause him, what he hopes to do to correct them, etc. If a person receives his own card, let him not reveal that, and merely role-play the situation as if it were that of someone else.
Variation
   I. Facilitator may list all the faults on the chalkboard or flipchart to graphically illustrate how many faults others have. This will serve to help participants realize that their faults are not so terrible and are probably shared by most others in the group.
  II. Facilitator may relate the old Hasidic saying that if everyone were able to put all his troubles and problems in a bag, and then everyone hang his bag on a tree, and then be able to select any bag he wished, the wise person would take his own bag.
Reference
Muriel Schiffman, **Self Therapy,** "Self Acceptance," pp. 118-120
Adapted from **Handbook for Facilitators,** mimeographed booklet of the Unitarian Church of Santa Barbara, California, 1971.

GOOD WHAT?—A self-Acceptance Game
Goals
    I. To foster self-acceptance
    II. To increase self-awareness and self-disclosure
Group Size
    Unlimited number of groups of six to eight
Time Required
    One hour
Materials
    None
Physical Setting
    Room with space for circles of eight
Process
    I. Facilitator asks groups to break into small groups of six to eight. He then explains that he will say a number of phrases beginning with the adjective "good." For example: good ball catcher, good swimmer, good driver. After each phrase, each person in small groups will have a chance to respond. They may say: a) yes, b) no, c) pass. If one feels he is a good swimmer (or whatever the particular phrase), he says Yes. If not, he says No. If uncertain, or if he prefers not to share on this question, he says Pass.
    II. Facilitator announces the phrase for each group to respond to, and gives them several minutes to give each person a turn to respond. He then announces another phrase, etc.
    III. After the groups have responded to six or eight such phrases, all beginning with "good," each group may discuss, with persons who responded "no" in particular explaining (if they wish) why they responded the way they did. Persons who responded "yes" may also volunteer to explain why they answered the way they did.
    IV. Each group may conclude with brief statements about what they learned, re-learned, discovered, or re-discovered about themselves.
Variation
    I. Group members may respond in written form to the "good" phrases and then share as they wish later.

        List of Suggested **GOOD WHAT?** Phrases

Good writer	Good parent
Good speaker	Good worker
Good sibling	Good friend
Good athlete	Good American
Good lover	Good singer
Good dancer	Good dreamer
Good neighbor	Good leader
Good organizer	Good artist
Good student	Good swimmer
Good dresser	Good citizen

This exercise comes from Tim Timmerman & Jim Ballard, **Strategies in Humanistic Education,** Vol. I, (Amherst, Mass.: Mandala, 1975), pp. 70-71.

ACCEPTING OUR WEAKNESS: I'm O.K. Just Like I Am

Goals
I. To stress the importance of accepting weakness and limitations as a prerequisite for high self-esteem
II. To demonstrate that all persons have stronger and weaker points and that the weaker points do not detract from one's overall OK-ness
III. To help persons admit weakness and limitations and not be ashamed of them

Group Size
Ten or more

Time Required
Thirty to sixty minutes

Materials
Pencil and paper, and some hard surface to write on such as a magazine or table

Physical Setting
Place for each member of the group to either sit on a chair at a table, or on the floor with a magazine to write on

Process
I. Facilitator explains that this exercise will focus on each of us as a finite and mortal creature. We all have weaknesses, shortcomings and limitations. If our ideal-self is too far from our real-self, the gap can create low self-esteem, frustration and discouragement. If we realize that being imperfect is human, and if we can accept our weaknesses, knowing that we are all doing the best we can for right now, our self-esteem will be improved. This exercise is designed to help us look at some of our weaknesses and stress the fact that these shortcomings do not make us any less worthwhile as human beings
II. Facilitator explains that each person will now write down three or four of the things he is most embarrassed about, his biggest failures or weaknesses, things he doesn't like about himself, but knows, nevertheless, are true
III. Each person finds a partner and discusses what he wrote, trying to be non-defensive and as self-accepting as possible.
IV. In groups of ten, each person in a circle should say the following sentence, mentioning the most serious or important weakness on his list: "I am...., (such as: a poor public speaker), and I am a very worthwhile person."
V. After each person has said that sentence, volunteers, or all participants, should describe their feelings during and after saying it. What implications are there for one's self-esteem?

Variations
I. Each person may select one glaring weakness of which he is a-shamed, or about which he is unhappy, and write it on a large piece of paper, taping it on his chest. Then group members mill around the room with a large, proud smile on the face. (The purpose of this is to de-sensitize persons to the shame they have over specific short-comings).

References

David R. Belgum, **What Can I Do About the Part of Me I Don't Like?** (Particularly designed to raise the self-esteem of physically handicapped persons, but applicable to all of us, since we are all to a greater or lesser degree handicapped with some physical or emotional weakness or limitation).

I learned this exercise from Elaine Elkins

TRUSTING YOUR ORGANISM: The Carrot-Eating Exercise

Goals

I. To experience the difference between integrating new things into one's body and gobbling them down (both ideas and food), and to relate these patterns to our self-esteem.

II. To compare physical and emotional patterns which reflect our self-esteem.

III. To help participants understand the meaning of "consulting one's gut" about new information and concepts.

Group Size

Any size group

Time Required

Thirty minutes

Materials

Several raw, cleaned, ready-to-eat carrots

Physical Setting

No special requirements

Process

I. Participants are given a small piece of carrot and told to eat it in their normal style. Then they are given another carrot and told to chew on it until is liquid and then swallow it.

II. Facilitator asks participants to describe how it was eating the carrot very slowly, and how they think it will be assimilated into the body. Volunteers in group respond.

III. Facilitator suggests to participants that eating styles are related to how we assimilate new ideas, new information, new concepts when we encounter them. In groups of four, participants compare their eating styles with the way they take in new ideas. Some may say, "I gobble it down quickly, without chewing, without assimilating—swallowing what others tell me 'whole.'" Others may chew it slowly, think carefully, before they accept it.

IV. Group may compare two eating styles, and what effects they have on the body—which will be integrated better. Implications for self-esteem can be discussed.

V. Facilitator then asks group to suggest what self concept a person who eats rapidly and/or swallows whole food and other new things—such as ideas and information. ("I am unworthy—I'll accept whatever they give me. I can not discriminate, I'll take it all in. I am incapable." Or: "I take care in what I integrate, what I assimilate. I can think on my own. I can discriminate. I am capable of deciding what to accept for myself and what to reject.")

Variations

I. Group may brainstorm ways in which we "swallow whole" the advice, morals, directions, ideas, of authority figures in society: church, newspapers, books, universities, popular culture, family, etc. Which "shoulds" have inhibited my own self-trust, trusting my own organism?

References

Fritz Perls, **Ego, Hunger and Aggression**

Adapted from an idea given me by Marie Fenton.

III. Real vs. Ideal Self
  Who Are You?
  Thumb Wrestling
  Childhood Visions of Myself
  The Image I Project
  First Impressions
  Apple Image
  Power of Imagery

WHO ARE YOU?

Goals

I. To help participants focus on their major strengths and characteristics

II. To encourage some self-introspection regarding the various roles one plays in life

III. To search for some of the important values and commitments each person has in life

Group Size

Twenty or more participants

Time Required

One hour

Materials

Pencil or pen and paper and hard surface to write on

Physical Setting

Place for each person to write

Process

I. Three volunteers are asked to leave the room. One at a time they are asked to return. When the first person returns, the facilitator asks: "Who are you?" When the person responds, the facilitator asks again, "Who else are you?" Following each answer, facilitator says: "And, in addition, who else are you?" This is repeated approximately ten times. If the answers are still flowing fairly rapidly and easily, the facilitator may want to continue beyond ten. It is during this deep self-searching, after the first easy answers, that really deep material will surface and more risky responses are likely to come out.

II. The second person is then invited in and the same procedure is repeated. Then the third.

III. Facilitator then asks each group member to write the answer to "Who Are You?" ten times. In other words, choose ten words which describe you. Volunteers then share what they have written.

Variation

I. If there is a person in the group who the facilitator feels has good ego strength and can handle a tough and risky exercise, he can press that person with the question fifteen or twenty times. After the person is tired and has exhausted the routine supply of superficial descriptions, the real essence of his inner being will be exposed. This might permit him to expose all of his strengths as well as weakness in a dramatic display of self-disclosure. This can be followed by group affection-giving (body lift, or non-verbal affection giving of various kinds) to demonstrate that the person is still warmly and unconditionally accepted by the group. Probably much more so than before, knowing what his deepest strengths and weaknesses are and having disclosed more of his inner self to the group.

Adapted from Simon, Howe and Kirschenbaum, **Values Clarification** (N.Y.: Hart, 1972), pp. 306-7.

THUMB WRESTLING: My Self Image as a Fighter, or Competer
Goals
I. To have participants experience their own assertion style
II. To have participants experience aspects of their behavior of various kinds and get feedback
Group Size
Ten or more people
Time Required
Thirty Minutes
Materials
None
Physical Setting
No special requirements
Process
I. Each person finds a partner, someone he does not know well. Dyad is told they will thumb wrestle and best out of three is winner. Facilitator demonstrates thumb wrestling. Dyads are sitting on floor, holding each other's hand with thumb up. At count of three they begin wrestling to see whose thumb can force other one down.

II. Facilitator tells each dyad to decide who will go first. After a minute or so, facilitator asks: How did each dyad decide who is going first? What does this say about your assertion style? What have you learned about yourself in this decision? How representative is this behavior of your general behaviors in other areas? How does my behavior in this instance reflect my self image? No verbal responses are made at this point.

III. Each dyad count to three at your own speed and begin thumb wrestling. Repeat three times. Facilitator then waits about ten to fifteen minutes for groups to finish their three bouts.

IV. Facilitator then poses the following questions to the entire group:
1) How important was it to you that you win?
2) Did you develop a strategy?
3) Did winner say anything to loser to make him/her feel better?
4) Did the loser say anything to himself to make him feel better?
5) Did each of you compare the size of your thumbs?
6) Did you let your partner win once to be nice?
7) Did fighting with a member of the opposite sex, if that is the case, change your attitude or your behavior?
Each dyad now spends about ten minutes sharing their answers to these questions.

V. Volunteers in group share some of the highlights of the experience.
Variations
I. For more intensive emotional involvement, some groups may choose to experience their assertion style through hand wrestling or foot wrestling, or other competitive experiences which they select.

References

George Bach and Herb Goldberg, **Creative Aggression**

Herbert Fensterheim and Jean Baer, **Don't Say Yes When You Want To Say No**

I learned this exercise from Jack Canfield.

CHILDHOOD VISIONS OF MYSELF: My Ideal Self

Goals
- I. To help participants recover their early vision of a core ideal self, dream of what they wanted to become and achieve in life.
- II. To encourage participants to re-own parts of themselves which may have become forgotten or repressed over the years.
- III. To encourage a fuller self-understanding of participants to better enable them to realize more of their potential.

Group Size
Ten or more

Time Required
Ninety minutes to two hours

Materials
Pen or pencil and paper

Physical Setting
Room large enough for each person to sit privately and write early vision of ideal self, and return to group circle.

Process
- I. Facilitator leads discussion on concept of ideal self image. Explains that each of us had a dream of what we wanted to be in life, what we wanted to contribute to humankind, our earliest dreams for ourselves. This is called our ideal-self core, and it usually exerts a powerful influence upon us growing up and even now. Recalling these early dreams and visions can prove extremely rewarding.
- II. Each person writes for fifteen minutes, using key words, or even pictures, of how he wanted himself to be as a child or adolescent. "What did I want to accomplish, to become? What did I most want to contribute in my early life? What was my dream for myself?"
- III. Volunteers share what they have written.
- IV. Group discussion on such questions as "What did this reowning of my early dreams and visions mean to me? What implications does it have for my life today? What actions might I take to change my life in a positive direction, based on this early dream, ideal-self core? What benefits did this exercise have for me? For the group?"

Variations
- I. Facilitator can give "homework assignment" at previous meeting to give thought to the early ideal-self core so as to be ready to write it down at next meeting, then following above steps.
- II. Guided fantasy can be used to dig into unconscious self-ideal image of childhood. Have person go into a room in the house in which he grew up, stare at himself in a full mirror, and picture himself as he wanted to be when he would reach adulthood. What hopes, accomplishments, dreams, did he consider at that early time in his life?
- III. Small group discussions may be held on the subject, "What visions of ideal self do I encourage in my children?"

References
Nathaniel Branden, **The Disowned Self**

Lorene A. Stringer, **The Sense of Self**
Bill & Carole Tegeler, **The People Press**
Adapted from Herbert Otto, **Group Methods to Actualize Human Potential.**
(Beverly Hills, Cal.: The Holistic Press, 1973), pp. 131-137.

THE IMAGE I PROJECT: How Do You See Me?

Goals
  I. To help group members get a clear objective view of the image they project to others, to line up their self-image with the group's image.
 II. Through clarifying one's projected image, to examine ways to change and improve the image.
III. To help establish a sense of trust and a climate of growth in a group that has been meeting for some time.

Group Size
Ten to twenty-five participants

Time Required
Approximately ten minutes per group member, or about two hours.

Materials
Pencil or pen and paper for each member

Physical Setting
A room large enough for group to sit in circle

Process
  I. Facilitator explains that the purpose of this exercise is to help members clarify the image they project to others. In short, how do others see me? Usually we infer this data indirectly from things people say, how they look at us, how they treat us, etc. This will be an opportunity to hear it directly for those who wish to. (Facilitator stresses voluntary nature of exercise).
 II. The first part of the exercise requires no group disclosure, and therefore all members can participate, whether or not they wish to volunteer later. Facilitator leads group discussion to achieve some rough consensus on a definition of what is an image projection. (Style of dress, appearance, use of body, voice, face, types of communication, strength, etc.) In addition to the individual components, there will usually be a composite picture, or Gestalt image, which a person projects.
III. Each person should now take ten minutes to write on his paper:
    A) What image do I project to others?
    B) How do I want to improve this image?
    Only those volunteering to do so will be asked to share their writing. Everyone, however, should make the description and desired change list, for his own benefit.
 IV. One person at a time approaches the center of the circle and addresses the group (taking responsibility for the feedback that follows): "What self-image do I project and how can I improve it?" Focus person may dialog with each person giving feedback, as he wishes. After the conclusion of the feedback that is voluntarily offered, the person may, if he wishes, share what he had written prior to the feedback. The focus person should ask one or two members to take notes for him, recording the feedback of group members while he listens to it so that he will have a record later.
  V. The focus person may share his feelings during the giving of feed-

84

back regarding his self-image at the end of his time in the center.

VI. After everyone who wishes to be focus person has done so, the group may wish to discuss "What were the value and learnings from this experience?"

References

Maxwell Maltz, **Self-Image Psychology**

Jerry Greenwald, **Be The Person You Were Meant To Be**

Adapted from Herbert Otto, **Group Methods to Actualize Human Potential.** (Beverly Hills, Cal.: The Holistic Press, 1973), pp. 118-121.

FIRST IMPRESSIONS
Goals
    I. To help participants become more aware of the initial impressions they make on others, and how these change after deeper relationships are developed.
    II. To help participants adjust their ideal self image with their real self image.
Group Size
From ten to twenty-five persons
Time Required
One hour
Materials
None
Physical Setting
Room large enough for participants to be seated in circle
Process
    I. Facilitator explains that part of the benefit of participating in a group training event is the feedback we receive from other members. This helps us to see ourselves more accurately. Not everything everyone else thinks and says may be useful to us. Often we may want to check out the feedback with others, in this group and elsewhere. Feedback has a cumulative effect, and if it is corroborated, may be very useful to us. With regard to our self image, it is important to know how others see us, and how we come across, especially in a new group. This exercise will help us achieve a sharper understanding of ourselves as others view us.
    II. Break into groups of eight or ten and each group is seated in a circle. Each person in the group who desires feedback asks the group to tell him how they perceived him the first time they encountered. This includes such questions as physical appearance, warmth, passive or aggressive, extrovert or introvert, secure or diffident, calm or nervous, etc. It will be most helpful to point out specific physical signs that disclose inner feelings and concrete behaviors which convey impressions to others. The more specific the feedback in terms of appearance and behavior, the more helpful it will be. Facilitator explains that for maximum benefit from this exercise, the focus person should not be defensive, but may ask clarifying questions.
    III. The group may now discuss what they learned from this exercise.
    IV. The group then continues the feedback in terms of how the initial impressions changed or were reinforced after the persons became more deeply acquainted.
Variation
    I. This exercise can be done early in the group's life and be limited to first impressions. Then, later, after a day or two, the same groups can reconvene to discuss what changes or reinforcements took place in these impressions.
    II. This exercise can be done at an early stage of the training event in groups of four which can then become permanent support groups to

reconvene to correct opinions on first impressions and to offer other feedback and support to one another as the training proceeds.

Reference

Sidney B. Simon, Howard Kirschenbaum and Leland Howe, **Values Clarification.**

AN APPLE IMAGE: Holding on to Self Image
Goals
  I. Convey the importance of how our self-image affects our behavior.
  II. Convey sense of difficulty one faces in changing his self-image.
  III. Experience how much one can learn about oneself through imagery.
Group Size
  Ten or more persons
Time Required
  Thirty minutes
Materials
  None
Physical Setting
  No special requirements
Process
  I. Facilitator asks each person to find a comfortable place to sit and relax. Tells group to close eyes and relax, letting all of the tension flow out of the body. Now hold out your right hand and hold an apple in it (apple is imaginary). Look at the apple (keeping eyes closed), examine it, feel it, get to know it.
  II. Facilitator continues: Open your eyes, still holding the apple. Trade your apple with someone sitting next to you. Look at your new apple. Compare it with the one you had before. Now trade back and get your own apple again.
  III. Facilitator now asks each person to consider the following questions and issues:
    1) How many people felt that the apple you started with was better than the one you received from your partner?
    2) How many were relieved to receive your own apple back?
    3) How many found it hard to dismiss the image you had of the apple even after the exercise? Or to change the image in your hand from your apple to your partner's apple?
    4) Did the trading and trading back, and the comparison between the apples tell you anything about your style of giving and receiving? Are you a person who gives more than he receives or vice versa?
  IV. Dyads discuss these questions among themselves for ten minutes.
  V. Lecturette/discussion on the importance of images and self-images. Facilitator may say something like: In a period of a minute or two you probably became strongly attached to your own apple, an image you created in a second. Many of you probably found it hard to dismiss and let go of the images you created for yourself. Compare this with the image of yourself which has been in the process of creation for many years. How difficult it is to change one's self-image! Also: how important it is that the self-image of a child and/or student be allowed to be a positive and healthy one. What a great responsibility parents and teachers have to facilitate the creation of a positive self-image in their charges! Once an image is stamped, it is not easily

changed. Nevertheless, it **can be changed.** It is only an **image,** a picture. A healthy understanding toward one's self-image is a combined realization of possible improvement with a realistic assessment of the difficulty involved and patience required in changing a long-standing mental image.

IV. Volunteers in group may comment and/or share their experiences in this exercise or in other areas.

References

Maxwell Maltz, **The Magic Power of Self-Image Psychology**

Robert Desoille, **The Directed Daydream**

Maurice Rapkin, **The Power of Pretend**

Robert DeMille, **Put Your Mother on the Ceiling**

I learned this exercise from Jack Canfield

THE POWER OF IMAGERY: Emotions, Behavior and Your Self-Image
Goals
   I. To demonstrate the effect mental images have on our feelings and behavior
Group Size
   Ten or more persons
Time Required
   Approximately thirty minutes
Materials
   None
Physical Setting
   No special requirements
Process
   I. Facilitator: Close your eyes, relax, and sit in a comfortable position. Imagine that you are now standing on the terrace of the top floor of the tallest skyscraper in the world. Now walk slowly over to the edge and look down. Stay with the feelings you now have for a few moments. Look up for a minute, and look down again at the area below. See what you find on the ground. Look up again. Now walk over to the other edge of the terrace, from which you can see the street that intersects the one you just watched. Look down there now. What are your feelings? Notice your breathing, your body reactions. Now slowly look up again, and take a few steps back.
   Slowly return to this room.
   II. Facilitator: Now ask yourself these questions:
      1) What were my emotional reactions?
      2) How did my breathing, heart-rate, gut feeling and body reactions respond to the imagined experience?
      3) What lessons can we derive from the influence this purely imaginary experience had on you? (Most people report mild to intense emotional reactions of fear, panic, rapid heart-beat, shallow breathing, butterflies, etc.).
   III. Now find a partner and discuss your emotional and physical reactions to this imaginary experience. What implications are there for self-image we hold of ourselves in terms of its effects on our thinking, our attitudes, our behavior, our feelings? Think of some ways in which your own self-image influences these things within you and your life. Share these with your partner.
   IV. Volunteers may share some highlights of the dyadic discussion in the total group.
Variations
   I. Think of other dangerous situations which might stir up emotions in specific people or groups you are dealing with, such as fighting in a war currently going on somewhere, undergoing a traumatic experience recently reported in a newspaper, to make the experience more current and personal.
I learned this experience from Jack Canfield.

IV. Raising Self Esteem
    Reaching For a High
    Centering
    No Matter What You Say
    Dual Personalities
    Expanding Self Concept
    Wise Old Person Fantasy

REACHING FOR A HIGH: A Fantasy Exercise

Goals

    I. To help participant identify a peak experience

    II. To develop a method to raise one's temporary mood of low self-esteem

Group Size

    Ten or more

Time Required

    Fifteen minutes

Materials

    None

Physical Setting

    A comfortable setting

Process

    I. Facilitator tells group to get comfortable, relax, let the tension flow out of your body, close your eyes. Use any one of several standard relaxation techniques.

    II. Think of a time when you were feeling especially good about yourself. Identify the scenery, the persons present, the time of day, what the weather was like. See if you can see the colors, smell the smells, get fully into the mood of that time and place.

    III. Enjoy being there and watch your self-esteem rise as you experience that scene and time.

    IV. When you are ready, come back slowly and open your eyes.

    V. Facilitator tells participants that any time they are feeling tired, bored, lack of energy, depressed, or in a mood of low self-esteem, during this workshop or on any other occasion, go to that spot in your fantasy and enjoy it. You will thus draw strength and energy, and be able to return refreshed and renewed.

I learned this exercise from Noel (Speed) Burch, of Effectiveness Training, Inc.

CENTERING: Self-Esteem and Balance
Goals
 I. To demonstrate the benefits of centering, of being on-balance
 II. To compare the wisdom of the physical organism with the wisdom of the psychic organism
 III. To transmit experientially the idea that a person with self-esteem is firmly based emotionally
Group Size
This exercise can be demonstrated with two people out front, or with the entire group participating.
Time Required
Fifteen to thirty minutes
Materials
No special materials required
Physical Setting
Preferably a room with a carpet
Process
 I. Facilitator asks group to divide into dyads. Both members of the dyad put hands face high, facing the partner, and partners touch the flat of each other's hands.
 II. One of partners is instructed to point his toes inward, pigeon-toe-like, with knees also facing in towards each other.
 III. Facilitator asks other partner to push on the hands of his partner who is pigeon-toed and try to push him off balance. (This should be fairly easily done with one good push, since the pigeon-toe position is unbalanced and awkward, and a person standing in that position is not well-balanced).
 IV. This time the person who was standing pigeon-toed now stands with feet pointing comfortably outward, in a firm, balanced position, with knees slightly bent, almost as if he were lifting weights on his shoulders and his shoes were nailed to the floor. From this balanced position it will be much more difficult for the partner to push him over.
 V. Facilitator instructs partner to push person who is standing with feet the new way and see if he can throw him off balance. (It will probably be more difficult, if not impossible, to be pushed over from this position of strength, and balance and centeredness.
 VI. Partners switch roles, and the partner who was pushing now stands in both positions and experiences the difference in being able to maintain his balance.
 VII. Facilitator now leads discussion to process the experience. What conclusions can be reached about our bodies and our emotions? One conclusion which the group will probably come to is that a person who is well-balanced, or centered, with his focus of strength within him, will not be easily toppled or shaken. A person with low self-esteem, whose centering, or self-balance, is not firm, will be thrown into anger, defensiveness, hostility, insecurity, by a slight attack or challenge. On the other hand, a person who is centered, who finds

his focus within, firmly balanced, will not easily be thrown off-balance or caught off-guard. Fritz Perls put it succinctly in **Gestalt Therapy Verbatim:** "Without a center, everything goes on in the periphery and there is no place from which to work, from which to cope with the world....This achieving the center, being grounded in one's self, is about the highest state a human can achieve." (p. 37) Nena and George O'Neil say this about centering:

Centering is the process of becoming aware of what **you** really want, how **you** really feel, what **you** really need. It is the process by which you come to know your essential self—your center of being which gives you a feeling of balance in life. Centering helps you to feel in place in life, and being centered is feeling confidence and security in yourself. (**Shifting Gears,** pp. 134-5).

Variations

I. Group can break into fours and each share ways in which they are centered and are not centered; how they have found centering useful in their lives; and when it might have helped at a time when they were not centered.

References

Nena and George O'Neill, **Shifting Gears** (Especially Chapter 7, "Centering and Focusing")

Frederick S. Perls, **Gestalt Therapy Verbatim**

Stephen A. Tobin, "Wholeness and Self-Support," in John O. Stevens (ed.), **Gestalt Is,** pp. 129-147.

Tony Banet, "Centering," **Annual Handbook for Group Facilitators,** 1977.

NO MATTER WHAT YOU SAY: An Exercise in Self-Strengthening

Goals
I. To strengthen the ego of the participant
II. To experience assertive response to put-downs
III. To teach methods of self-validation
IV. To experience ego self-defense in the safety of the group

Group Size
Fifteen or more participants

Time Required
Ten minutes

Materials
No special materials required

Physical Setting
No special requirements

Process
I. To introduce the experience, the facilitator explains that the society in which we live is accustomed to use put-downs very frequently. Persons have been taught to build themselves by tearing others down. This is especially true in authority positions, in which bosses or other persons in positions of power will deride or ridicule others. Often members of a family do it to each other.

II. The facilitator will shout put-downs at the group (tailored to the age, sex, race, religion, and/or other special characteristics of the group). After each one, the group will say in unison: "No matter what you say or do to me, I'm still a worthwhile person."

III. Facilitator asks group to practice saying that line a few times together, asking them to say it louder and louder each time. After two or three times, he then shouts at them some insult, such as "This is the dumbest group I've ever worked with!" The group then responds automatically, "No matter what you say or do to me, I'm still a worthwhile person." Facilitator continues to shout insults appropriate to the group, trying to think of the commonly held stereotypes and degrading images cast upon them by the public, government or other groups, institutions and individuals.

(For example, with a group of humanistic educators, the facilitator would shout: "Do you call that touchy-feely stuff education?" Or: "Stop teaching my kids that garbage and get back to the three R's!!!!")

IV. For minority group self concept strengthening, the facilitator would shout common stereotypes expressed by prejudiced people against the minority group.

References
Lou Benson, **Images, Heroes and Self-Perceptions.** Chapter Three, "The Put-Down."
I learned this exercise from Jack Canfield

DUAL PERSONALITIES: Feeling Low and Feeling High

Goals
  I. To help participants become aware of the fluctuating nature of self-esteem
  II. To enable participants to identify their own moods of high and low self-esteem
  III. To identify triggers or causative circumstances which tend to bring on moods of high or low self-esteem

Group Size
Preferably ten or more

Time Required
One to two hours

Materials
Pencil or pen and paper

Physical Setting
Comfortable place to sit and write

Process
  I. Facilitator explains that self-esteem fluctuates, sometimes dramatically, within each person, often even during the course of the same day. During this exercise we will try to identify these experiences and attempt to get some control over them.
  II. Facilitator asks each person to take a sheet of paper and draw a line down the middle. On one side write the ways you feel, think, and act when you are feeling low about yourself. On the other side, the ways you feel, think and act when you feel especially good about yourself. Be very specific.
  III. Try to look upon these two moods as two parts of yourself or two personalities. Use your imagination and give each of these two personalities a name which in some ways summarizes or symbolizes these two moods.
  IV. Share in groups of four what you have written so far.
  V. Now try to identify for yourself what types of situations, experiences, persons or events have an effect on raising or lowering your self-esteem. What are the times, places, etc. which generally cause you to feel good about yourself and bad about yourself. Try to be as specific and concrete as you can.
  VI. Share these with the group and have the group brainstorm and use fantasy to suggest what other ways there might be for each person to raise his self-esteem.
  VII. Share reactions to this experience and what you learned about your own self-esteem.

Variation
  I. Contrast in dyads how each partner can increase the proportion of your life during which you have higher self-esteem.

Adapted from Martin L. Seldman & David Hermes, **Personal Growth Thru Groups:** A Collection of Methods (San Diego: The We Care Foundation, Inc., 1975), pp. 17-25.

EXPANDING YOUR SELF CONCEPT: A Risk-Taking Exercise

Goals

  I. To convey the idea that our mental image of ourselves, our self concept, can be a limiting factor in our behavior.
  II. To give participants the experience, in a safe, laboratory environment, to experience new limits and widened boundaries for their previously limited self concepts.
  III. To encourage moderate and prudent risk-taking as a way to expand self concept and experiment with new behaviors as new aspect of one's daily living.

Group Size

Individual or group of any size

Time Required

Whatever length of time it takes to carry out the risk-taking fully and get into the feelings accompanying the risking behavior, and process the experience, individually or in a group.

Materials

Pencil and paper

Physical Setting

Exercise can be done anywhere, according to the needs of the specific risk-taking behavior

Process

  I. Facilitator explains that fear of doing some specific behavior is a symptom that our self concept limit has been reached. Expanding the previous limits of our repertoire of behaviors is a freeing and expanding experience, often creating euphoric feelings of high self-esteem. One should be able to choose his behaviors on the basis of will, not of fear.
  II. Facilitator asks members to write down five things which he is afraid to do, such as: singing in public, speaking back to someone important, dressing loudly or ostentatiously, doing a dance, calling a certain friend or client, kissing someone, etc. Explain that the participant will be able to choose from among this list and need not be limited to the original five. In fact, the more scary these five are, the better. Allow several minutes.
  III. Participants are to now select one of these behaviors that can be done in the group, or in the room where the group is, within a five minute range of time, using facilities and materials available. (If all five behaviors are impossible in the here-and-now setting, participant may come up with another one).
  IV. Carry out the behaviors that can be done simultaneously, with as many in the group taking part at the same time as possible. Then have members who must have the attention of the entire group, or several others, carry out their risky behaviors. Facilitator should encourage high risk behaviors by saying that this is a supportive environment in which we can take risks we would not be inclined to do outside the group. Furthermore, the higher the risk you take, the

higher others in the group will be inclined to take. Thus, your risky behavior not only helps you but others in the group as well.

V. Have each member of the group explain what he did, and why it was risking and scary, and how it felt doing it.

Variation

I. This exercise can be done by an individual by himself.

II. Exercise can be done by one individual in a group who the group leader thinks would be helped by taking a risky step in the group.

III. Risky behaviors can be assigned as "homework" for growth and therapy groups. This widens the possible areas of natural behaviors in the back-home setting. Member should then report to group in next session.

IV. For persons or groups reluctant or slow in coming up with a list of risky behaviors, guided fantasy can be used to generate such a list, and get at the deeper fears which a person may not be able to think of consciously.

V. For those skilled in self-hypnosis or hypnosis, these techniques can be utilitized to help person get over initial fears of carrying out particularly risky behaviors.

WISE OLD PERSON FANTASY

Goals
  I. To enable participants to reach into their inner wisdom, or "higher self," to find ways to raise their self-esteem.
  II. To encourage participants to take responsibility for their own personal growth in the area of self-esteem.

Group Size
  Ten or more

Time Required
  Thirty minutes

Materials
  None

Physical Setting
  Comfortable setting for participants to sit or lie with space around them to stretch and relax.

Process
  I. Facilitator explains that this exercise is a guided fantasy in which participants will be able to call upon their own higher wisdom.
  II. Facilitator asks participants to sit back, relax, take a few deep breaths to center within themselves, and close their eyes. Facilitator then instructs group to picture themselves in their imagination to be in a large, open beautiful meadow. Look around the meadow and see the trees and grass and flowers. Smell the aroma of the meadow. Now walk towards a mountain beyond the meadow, and slowly ascend the mountain. At the top you see a building in which there is a large elevated throne with a wise old person sitting on it. Slowly you approach the wise old person and ask this question: What do I need to do to raise my self-esteem? (Facilitator pauses for several minutes for participants to hear their response).
  III. When you have heard your reply, turn around, realizing that you can always return, walk down the mountain, back through the meadow, and when you are ready, come back to this room and open your eyes.
  IV. Share in small groups of four the answers given by the wise old person.
  V. A few volunteers may share their replies with the entire group. (Some may wish to focus momentarily on the sex of the wise old person and any implications of this).

Variation
  I. Participants may symbolize their reply into a sign, picture, or symbol and draw it with pen or crayon, and then share with the small group.

Reference
  Martha Crampton, "The Use of Mental Imagery in Psychosynthesis," **Journal of Humanistic Psychology,** Fall, 1969.

THE THREE V'S: Vulture, Viper, Validation
Goals
   I. To raise group consciousness regarding self- and member-validation and put-downs.
   II. To encourage validation of fellow members and discourage put-downs during group discussion.
Group Size
   Any size group
Time Required
   Fifteen minutes to any time
Materials
   None
Physical Setting
   A room large enough for group to sit comfortably in a circle on the floor or on chairs
Process
   I. Facilitator asks group to discuss each other, a la encounter. Discuss feelings and stay in the here and now. Be honest and responsible for your own behavior.
   II. Facilitator gives instructions regarding three V's:
      1) Each time a member says something or does something (including non-verbal gestures with hands, face, and/or body,) which is seen by other member or members as a put-down to oneself, the objecting member will raise his hand with two fingers (index and middle of either hand) slightly curved forward like two ears of a vulture, and make an ugly noise such as **gawk, gawk** from back of throat. Facilitator illustrates. Objecting members point this vulture-V toward person accused of using a put-down of self.
      2) Each time a person says something or uses verbal or non-verbal behavior which is seen by others as a put-down to someone else in the group, objecting member(s) will make a V with the same fingers, making the V horizontal, as if flat on a table, with the index finger of the other hand between the prongs of the V, simulating a snake's tongue, and make the sound SSSSSSS as a snake (viper). Facilitator illustrates, showing and explaining how a put-down comment or behavior is snake-like.
      3) Each time a person validates himself or another, a V sign is held up, similar to a V for victory. This V stands for validation. Facilitator illustrates and explains that this reward will encourage validating comments during group discussion. No sound accompanies this V.
   III. Facilitator asks group to engage in encounter-type discussion for 15 minutes, with all group members watching for opportunities to use the three V hand-signals to accuse persons who put down themselves or others, and encourage others to validate themselves and others.

IV. After fifteen minutes of discussion, discuss the feelings of those who used any of the three V's or were the target or object of others who used them.

Variation

I. This strategy can be suggested to any group which is discussing personal values or issues to encourage validation and discourage put-downs.

II. The three Vs can be used by any group assembled for a variety of purposes, such as a weekend retreat or encounter, or whatever else.

Reference

This structured experience is based on the three V strategy in Values Clarification created by Sidney B. Simon, now fully elaborated in his small paperback book, **Vulture** (Argus, 1977).

NURTURING RELATIONSHIPS

Goals

   I. To transmit importance of participants as nurturing persons who influence self-esteem of many others.

   II. To help participants become more sensitive to their own power to raise self-esteem in significant others.

Group Size

   Unlimited number of dyads

Time Required

   Thirty minutes

Materials

   None

Physical Setting

   No special requirements

Process

   I. Facilitator explains that this exercise is designed to help participants get in touch with their powers as agents of nurture and high self-esteem for others. Facilitator asks participants to think of a person in their early lives who nurtured them, cared for them, gave them a lot of affection and esteem: a neighbor, an aunt, grandparent, teacher, etc., someone other than a parent. Someone who influenced your life in your early growing years. Share in small groups.

   II. Now think of some people over whom you exercise this influence, someone who looks to you for guidance and love; someone over whom you have influence and for whom you are, or can be, a nurturing agent, and a force for high self-esteem. Share in small groups how you can become more influential in the life of this person.

   III. Facilitator summarizes by saying that we all have enormous power to influence the lives of others, and especially the self-esteem of those in our charge, such as children, young relatives, students, employees, colleagues, clients, patients, etc. We should recognize our power as agents of helping people achieve high self-esteem.

THE CHEERLEADER VALIDATION

Goals

I. To experience group esteem and affection

II. To experience mass validation, as from a large audience

Group Size

Works best with at least 25 participants

Time Required

Ten to fifteen minutes

Materials

None

Physical Setting

Can be done very effectively indoors or outdoors

Process

I. Group forms a circle and one volunteer goes into center

II. Focus person yells out his name like a cheerleader

III. Group yells out as a chorus of assistant cheerleaders, RA, RA, RA (three times), then breaks out in applause

IV. Focus person may tell how this felt

Variation

I. This is an activity which can be done by families. Facilitator may point out to participants that they may do this at home. If family groups attend a lab, they can carry out this exercise for a member of the family.

I learned this exercise from Lee Innocenti

STRENGTH BOMBARDMENT

Goals

I. To help a person recognize his capabilities and potential

II. To experience deserved positive feedback from the group

Group Size

Eight to fifteen participants is optimal, although larger groups can use this structured experience

Time Required

Thirty to sixty minutes, depending on size of group

Materials

No special materials

Physical Setting

Group should be sitting in a circle comfortably

Process

I. Facilitator explains that modern research shows that persons are frequently not aware of their capabilities, strengths, potentialities. This exercise will help each focus person become more aware of his own strengths as seen by the group.

II. Each person takes a turn to become focus person. He can go into the center, or remain in his place. The group takes turns giving the focus person deserved positive feedback, focusing solely on the strengths of the focus person. The focus person is told to "drink in" in the positive comments of the group, and to be careful not to deny, "discount", minimize, or in any way qualify these strength descriptions. Rather, he should practice the skill of letting in, and "owning" this complimentary information.

Variations

I. The group can be divided into small groups of four, with each of the four members receiving deserved positive feedback from the other three. This saves considerable amount of time in groups of 16 to 20.

II. Instead of using sentences and descriptions of the focus person's strengths, the group may yell at the focus person adjectives, one or two word descriptions—such as: strong, compassionate, gentle, understanding, handsome, good speaker, talented artist, etc.

References

Herbert Otto, **A Guide to Developing Your Potential**

Gardner Murphy, **Human Potentialities**

A TIME TO THROW STONES

Goals

I. To foster awareness of the effects of put-downs

II. To sensitize participants to potential dangers in careless behavior

Group Size

Unlimited

Time Required

Thirty to forty-five minutes

Materials

Chalk and chalkboard or magic marker and flipchart

Physical Setting

A room large enough for participants to sit or lie comfortably for a fantasy exercise

Process

I. Facilitator asks group to get comfortable, relax, let the tension flow out of the body, and close eyes, readying themselves for a guided fantasy.

II. Take yourself back to your childhood and see the house you grew up in. Look around and see the scenery, neighboring houses and sites, smell the smells, hear the noises of your childhood neighborhood. Now see yourself inside the house and look around at the furniture and the rooms. Think of a time in that house when someone humiliated you, or put you down, or made you feel small and unworthy. (Allow five minutes for this to come into vision). Feel the feelings of that moment and perhaps some of the pain and humiliation. Stay with it for a short while, and when you are ready, slowly open your eyes and return to the group.

III. Facilitator asks the group to describe their feelings at the time of being humiliated or put down, and list these on the chalkboard or flipchart. After ten or fifteen are listed, a few volunteers may relate their stories briefly.

IV. A brief discussion can follow on the perils of putting others down, and the long-lasting negative effects.

Variation

I. Group may break up into small groups of four and talk about ways in which each member is prone to put down certain people in their lives and how they intend to change these patterns.

References

Dorothy Corkille Briggs, **Your Child's Self-Esteem**

Kaoru Yamamoto, **The Child and His Image**

Haim Ginott, **Between Parent and Child**

I APPRECIATE: A Validation Exercise
Goals
    I. To encourage an atmosphere of warmth and validation within the group
    II. To sensitize participants to the many possible ways of validating others and self
    III. To model an atmosphere of raising self-esteem of those close to us
Group Size
Unlimited number of groups of ten
Time Required
Twenty to thirty minutes
Materials
No special materials required
Physical Setting
    I. Group members stand in a circle with arms of each on the shoulders of those to left and right
    II. A good beginning to this exercise might be a brief song or chant. (Example: Ohm). A quiet and emotional tone is thereby set for what follows.
    III. Facilitator explains that this exercise is to share appreciations of each other to foster group unity, trust and warmth.
    IV. Facilitator begins, providing two or three examples. He starts by saying: "I appreciate...." For example, "I appreciate Mary for helping me explain a point earlier this morning." Or: "I appreciate Howard for extending himself to Frank when Frank appeared to need some help and support."
    V. Group members will usually pick up the style very quickly and continue to send appreciation messages to other group members. This can continue for quite a long time. Sometimes a few moments of silence will permit members to think of other appreciations. The facilitator should not necessarily interpret a brief silence as a time to cut off the exercise. Rather he should give it time to develop into a long flow of love and care and appreciation. Givers of appreciation should speak directly to the person receiving the validation, and the receiver may not return a validation immediately after receiving one.
I learned this exercise in a Re-evaluation Counseling Group led by Carl Struever in Rochester, New York.

KILLER STATEMENTS: Identifying Put-Downs
Goals
  I. To identify common put-down statements
  II. To feel the effects of killer statements
  III. To become aware of how participant uses put-downs
Group Size
Ten or more
Time Required
Fifteen to thirty minutes
Materials
Pen or pencil and paper; chalk and chalkboard—or magic marker and newsprint or flipchart
Physical Setting
Room for entire group to see chalkboard or flipchart
Process
  I. Facilitator introduces exercise by explaining the harmful consequences of put-downs and killer statements and gestures. Children particularly are damaged by put-downs, but persons of all ages suffer from them.
  II. Facilitator asks group to brainstorm all the common killer statements that invalidate a person for a new idea, or for risking a personal statement or for displaying an emotion. Members can first generate their own list, and then have one or two persons write them down on the board as members call them out.
  III. Discuss in small groups how we have used killer statements and gestures against others, and how they have been used against us.
  IV. Discuss in small groups some of the killer statements and gestures that we experienced during our growing up years and what effects these have had on us.
  V. Think of some killer statements that you might have made recently, to a relative, neighbor, employe, friend, etc., and what effects it might have had on that person or on your relationship with that person.
Variation
  I. When the facilitator yells "Go," group members stand up and yell out several of the killer statements as forcefully as they possibly can. They then discuss how they felt, and process the experience. What mood was created in the room?
  II. Different members may volunteer to go to the front of the group and say something risky. Then have the group shout killer statements and make similar invalidating gestures. Then focus person shares his feelings during this experience.

Adapted from Jack Canfield and Harold Wells, **100 Ways to Enhance Self Concept in the Classroom** (Englewood Cliffs, N.J.: Prentice-Hall, 1976), pp. 67-68.

108

TOAST: A Closure Exercise
Goals
    I. To create an opportunity for appropriate closure
    II. To conclude a unit of training, or an entire training event, with an experience related to an important theme of the training event, validation.
Group Size
From ten to twenty-five, or sub-groups of ten to twenty-five
Time Required
45 to 60 minutes
Materials
One paper cup for each participant
Physical Setting
A room large enough for each individual to be seated in a circle, or if there are more than 25 participants, room for several circles.
Process
    I. Each person receives a paper cup. Facilitator explains that in order to bid farewell we are going to toast one another. However, this will be a symbolic toast. Our cups will not be filled with liquid, but with the human essence of each other.
    II. Facilitator gives an example, by modeling a toast. For example, "I toast you, Joe, and I put into my cup some of your courage to risk and grow."
    III. Facilitator then explains that this is the end of the day (event), and many, or most, of us will probably never see each other again. If we do, it will never be the same. Whether we see each other or not, it will be good if we can each take something away from our person-to person encounter. So let us toast each other, and as we do so, tell the person you are toasting what quality or characteristic or talent you want to take from him, and put it into your cup, and integrate that part of him into yourself. We will thus fill our cups with the essence of each other. Each of us has things which others can take from him and make it his own. Let us now toast one another.
    IV. Volunteers then toast each other randomly, at will, and take from each other whatever qualities they admire, thus filling their cups with the essence of the members of the group.
Variation
    I. In larger groups, break into groups of ten to fifteen, and each person will have an opportunity to take something of essence of each other person present to fill his cup as each person in the group toasts every other person.
I learned this exercise from Lee Innocenti.

THREE UNIQUE THINGS: A Self-Validation Exercise
Goals
    I. To help participants discover their own uniqueness
    II. To give participants practice in self-validation
    III. To create a sense of greater intimacy in the group
Group Size
Ten or more participants preferably
Time Required
Thirty to forty-five minutes
Materials
Pencil or pen and paper
Physical Setting
Comfortable place to write and for small groups to meet
Process
    I. Facilitator explains that each person is a unique creature. There never has been anyone like you and there never will be again. This exercise is to help you get in touch with the unique things about yourself. Everyone has some qualities, experiences, attributes, training, skills, or whatever that are relatively unique. All of these together produce YOU, a unique creation.
    II. Each person writes three to five things which are relatively unusual or unique to him. These things need not be absolutely idiosyncratic, just things that in all likelihood no one else in the group has done, learned, experienced, become, etc. For example, one woman who did this exercise said she slid down a slide into the Guatemala Canal. Another person studied ten years training to become a monk and two weeks before ordination changed his mind. The examples need not be that dramatic. A simple way to pose the question is: What unusual things have you learned or done?
    III. After writing a few things, form groups of four and share. One person from each group then shares with the entire group.
    IV. Facilitator may then lead a discussion about the lessons derived from the exercise. What implications are there to our uniqueness?
Variation
    I. In a group of twenty to twenty-five, break into dyads, and each person can tell the group about his partner's unique things. This can be a good break-the-ice and community-building exercise.
    II. Another way to use this is to talk about several unique things relating to my family.

COAT OF ARMS: Developing Human Potential
Goals
    I. To identify specific areas of ability and achievement in greater detail
    II. To develop experience in self-assessment of strengths
    III. To develop experience in self-validation
Group Size
No minimum required
Time Required
Thirty minutes
Materials
Pen, pencil or magic marker and paper
Physical Setting
Comfortable space to write and/or draw
Process
    I. Facilitator explains that many people do not realize their own strengths and they need to "take inventory."
    II. Facilitator explains that one way to do this is to fill out a "personal coat of arms," inventorying one's strengths, talents and abilities. The Personal Coat of Arms should be done in symbols, signs or drawings, rather than in words, except for item number 6.
    III. In space #1, draw a sign or symbol which indicates your strengths as a friend. In space #2, your strengths and talents as a member of your family, or other group. In space #3, draw a sign or symbol which represents your strengths in your work or job. In space #4, your strengths in sports (even if you're not inclined to active sports, there is something you can identify which you do well). In space #5, draw a sign or symbol which represents something positive about your appearance. Finally, in space #6, write three words which summarize the things you like best about yourself.
    IV. Share these in groups of four.
    V. One or more volunteers from each group of four can tell of one or two highlights in their group or from their own Personal Coat of Arms.
    VI. Make "I learned...." statements.
Variations
    I. Facilitator may select specific areas of talents and strengths depending on the age, special interests, vocational specialities, etc. of a particular group.
    II. As a community-building exercise, participants can hold up their coat-of-arms and mill around the room, sharing with anyone they meet.
    III. Another possibility for one of the spaces: two successes you had this past year.
    IV. Connect all of the spaces to family-related matters.
    V. Hang coat-of-arms on the wall, identified by name.
Reference
Herbert A. Otto, **Developing Your Potential**

PERSONAL COAT-OF-ARMS

1 2

3 4

5 6

BOAST: An Exercise in Self-Validation
Goals
  I. To provide experience in self-validation
  II. To help participants become more aware of their assets
  III. To help overcome inhibitions and societal ban on boasting
Group Size
Done best with fifteen or more
Time Required
Fifteen to thirty minutes
Materials
A copy of the poem, "Boast" by Stanley Herman (**Glad To Be Me**)
Physical Setting
A room large enough for people to mill around
Process
  I. Facilitator explains that society has taught us that boasting and talking nicely about ourselves is vain and unseemly. Actually, being aware of our strengths is not immodest but necessary. What is offensive to people is the person who does nothing but boast about himself, covering his own insecurity and often putting-down others in the process of boasting.
  II. Facilitator reads Stanley Herman's poem, "Boast," from **1972 Annual Handbook for Group Facilitators,** ed. John E. Jones and J. William Pfeiffer, p. 219 (quoted in **Glad To Be Me**).
  III. Facilitator explains that on the given signal each participant will walk around the room, and stop people, and boast about something he can do well. For example, a person might begin by saying, "Wow, am I a great... (pianist)!" The facilitator should demonstrate one such boasting sentence, and say it with gusto, pride, and vigor.
  IV. Facilitator can then lead a group discussion on how this exercise felt, and what personal learnings emerged from it.
Reference
Harvey Jackins, "Complete Appreciation of Self," in **The Human Situation,** pp. 45-58.
I learned this exercise from Lee Innocenti.

HOW PERCEPTIVE YOU ARE!—Learning to Accept Praise

Goals
I. To help participants become accustomed to accepting praise and compliments rather than discounting them.
II. To practice validating others.

Group Size
Unlimited number of dyads

Time Required
Ten to twenty minutes

Materials
None

Physical Setting
Comfortable place for dyads to talk privately.

Process
I. Find a partner and decide who will go first. A validates B and B replies with a broad smile, "How perceptive you are!" If B's statement is not convincing, A may ask him to repeat it until it is stated loud, clear and proudly.
II. Reverse and repeat.
III. A validates B in another quality and B says: "Yes, and not only that but...." (adding still another validation about himself).
IV. Reverse and repeat.
V. Dyads discuss with each other how they felt validating, being validated, and responding in the way indicated, rather than the usual discounting.
VI. Group discussion about how it was for participants and common feelings appearing in group.

Variation
I. Facilitator can suggest fixed compliments for A's to say to B's, such as "What a fantastic person you are" with B replying, "How perceptive you are!"
II. This can be repeated with many other such compliments, particularly ones related to the specific group of participants.
III. Groups of four can select a particular validation for each member and then have that one used in the dyadic exchange—one that the group member would feel most uncomfortable about hearing and accepting. For example, if a person sings well and is reticent to sing publicly, his dyadic partner would say: "What a beautiful singer you are!" and the person would reply, "How perceptive you are."
IV. Participants may be encouraged to practice this exercise with their families at home.

I learned this exercise from Sidney B. Simon.

PROUD WHIP: Self-Validation Training
Goals
    I. To help participants become more aware of their positive qualities and behaviors, and to feel better about themselves.
    II. To give participants practice in self-validation as a life-process.
    III. To help participants overcome shyness and reticence regarding their own strengths and positive achievements.
    IV. To help foster a climate of friendship in the group.
Group Size
    Ten or more
Time Requirement
    Twenty to thirty minutes
Materials
    None required
Physical Setting
    No special requirements
Process
    I. Facilitator explains that we often do many good, interesting, and/or significant things in our life which we take for granted. By recalling some of these things and sharing them in the group, we strengthen our good feelings about ourselves in terms of the things and values in life which we cherish. This should not be seen as undue bragging or boasting, but rather as confidently announcing some things we believe in or are happy about in our behavior.
    II. Each person in group announces something he is proud of in relation to himself. Specific topics may be: Something I'm proud of as a husband, as a father, as a sibling, as a friend, in my work, in my community, as a growing person, etc., etc. Possibilities are endless. Facilitator may leave the area open or may specify pride in some particular area of life. Each person should be given a chance to speak, but anyone who wishes may pass.
    III. Group may wish to discuss how it feels to validate oneself in front of a group, and what values and learnings it may have for them.
Variations
    I. Participants may be asked to go back in their lives and think of something they are proud of which they accomplished before age 15 or in other specific ages or areas of their lives.
    II. This exercise can be used after the group has met for several times by having each person talk about something he is proud of which he did during the life of the group. Or something I did today, or this week.
References
    Sidney B. Simon et al., **Values Clarification,** pp. 134-137.
    Robert C. Hawley & Isable L. Hawley, **Human Values in the Classroom,** pp. 223-235.
    Harvey Jackins, "The Complete Appreciation of Oneself" in **The Human Situation,** pp. 45-58.

POEM ABOUT ME

Goals
  I. To foster self-awareness and self-appreciation
  II. To validate oneself in a creative way

Group Size
  Can be done by an individual or group of any number

Time Required
  One hour

Materials
  Pen or pencil and paper

Physical Setting
  Comfortabie place for each participant to sit and write

Process
  I. Facilitator explains that a good way to tap the lower levels of our consciousness is to use our creative, imaginative powers in creative expression. When we sit down to write or draw, often things emerge which are not fully available to our conscious awareness. This exercise will help us tap this rich resource.
  II. Each person is asked to write a poem about himself. It can be in any form, rimed or unrimed, with poetic structure or just free flowing stream of consciousness. The poem may deal with a specific theme about our present or past life, or our future hopes, dreams or expectations. There is no limit or qualification to this poem, except that it be "About Myself."
  III. Share poems in groups of four.
  IV. Volunteers from each group of four may share their poem with the entire group.
  V. Return to groups of four and discuss what I learned about myself and what I can apply to help improve my self image.

Variation
  I. Other forms of creativity can achieve the same end—such as a painting "About Me," or a sculpture, or a prayer, or a song. Facilitator can assign everyone to work in the same medium, or ask each person to select the creative medium which appeals to him at the moment, or in which he feels most comfortably working.

SELF-ESTEEM TREE
Goals
    I. To help participants identify their strengths, abilities, talents, accomplishments and successes.
    II. To provide experiences in validating self and others.
Group Size
    No limits
Time Required
    Thirty minutes
Materials
    Pen, pencil, crayon or magic marker; copy of "Self-Esteem Tree."
Physical Setting
    Place for each participant to sit comfortably and draw and write
Process
    I. Facilitator explains importance of getting in touch with our strengths and resources, abilities and talents. On the roots of the Self-Esteem Tree asks participants to write in all of their talents and abilities. Leave some spaces to add more later.
    II. Facilitator then suggests that not only should we be more aware of our strengths and talents, but of the many successful things we have done. He then asks members to write on the branches of the Tree all of the things they have done successfully. Leave some branches empty for later additions.
    III. Participant then writes his name on the space provided on the tree trunk and all the Trees are posted on the wall. Other strengths and accomplishments can be added by oneself or others during the course of the workshop. Participants then get to take home their Tree at the end of the lab and display it prominently on the refrigerator. Perhaps other members of the family will then be encouraged to make their own Self-Esteem Tree.
Variations
    I. Instead of words, participants can draw symbols or signs representing their talents and accomplishments. This sometimes helps people reach more deeply into the lower layers of their consciousness.
    II. At the end of each workshop session, each person can whip around the circle and add one item to his tree, and then go and write or draw it on the posted Tree.
    III. Participants can share the contents of their Self-Esteem Trees by taping it on their chest and milling around the room, stopping to look at each other's, or just sharing in dyads or groups of four.
Adapted from Leland W. Howe and Mary Martha Howe, **Personalizing Education,** (N.Y.: Hart, 1975), pp. 97-98.

A SELF-ESTEEM TREE

THIS SELF-ESTEEM
TREE BELONGS TO

AN AD FOR YOURSELF

Goals

I. To help participants make an assessment of their strengths

II. To encourage participants to comfortably validate themselves publicly

III. To sharpen one's perspective on his own positive qualities

Group Size

Works best in a group of ten or more

Time Required

45 to 60 minutes

Materials

Pencil or pen and paper, and something to lean on for writing

Physical Setting

A room with a place to write

Process

I. Facilitator describes the advertisements that sometimes appear in magazines such as **Saturday Review** placed by lonely individuals seeking a mate. Suggests to group that they imagine themselves in that position having to restrict the ad to 13 words to save money.

II. Participants then write "I'm...." followed by 12 adjectives—one word each.

III. Share in groups of four to six.

IV. One volunteer from each group can share with the entire group.

V. In small groups, each member may then discuss the one quality on his list which was hardest for him to write; and/or the hardest one to share with others.

Variation

I. If you had to write the ad with only six words, which six adjectives would you delete, and which ones leave?

II. Going further, if you could only choose two words, which ones would you pick?

MY OBITUARY: How I Hope Others Will See Me

Goals

    I. To help participant focus on his present and potential strengths and accomplishments.

    II. To help participant see, from the perspective of his imagined death, the aspects of his life which he values and wants to work on, to continually improve his sense of accomplishment and self-esteem.

Group Size

Ten or more is optimum

Time Required

30 to 60 minutes

Materials

Pencil or pen and paper and something to lean on while writing

Physical Setting

A place where people can write comfortably

Process

    I. Facilitator explains that this exercise will help participants focus on their life from the perspective of their imagined death. It should be handled matter-of-factly in order not to raise the level of anxiety. Each participant is asked to write an obituary the way he would like it to appear in the daily paper when he dies. Presume that the death will take place in five years from the date of writing, and write it as of that time. For example, if today is March 1, 1982, date the obituary and write it as if the person died March 1, 1987.

    II. The facilitator can suggest some of the items to be included in the obituary, such as: cause of death, organizational affiliations, survivors, projects working on at time of death, major accomplishments, outstanding human qualities, some unrealized goals, arrangements for body, charitable contributions which can be made in his honor and others.

    III. Group breaks into small groups of four and shares their obituaries.

    IV. One person from each group of four can read his obituary.

Variation

    I. Participants may prefer to write the obituary as of the present moment, rather than five years hence. Or, perhaps ten or twenty years hence.

    II. In groups of four, participants can make a self-contract to designate which of the as-yet unaccomplished achievements or qualities can be realized within six months to a year, and have someone witness it and keep a copy.

Adapted from Simon, Howe & Kirschenbaum, **Values Clarification** (N.Y.: Hart, 1972), pp. 311-313.

VII. Group Caring and Validation
　　　Massage Train
　　　Car Wash
　　　Body Lift
　　　Caring Lift
　　　Group Applause
　　　Non-verbal Feedback

MASSAGE TRAIN: Mutual Back Rub
Goals
   I. To observe effects of massage techniques on self-esteem
  II. To express group caring
 III. To achieve team building effects
Group Size
  At least fifteen or more
Time Required
  Ten to twenty minutes
Materials
  None
Physical Setting
  Room in which group can make a large circle
Process
   I. Group forms a large circle. Facilitator asks everyone to turn to the right and put his hands on the shoulders of the person next to him. Facilitator says: Bring some comfort and caring to these tired shoulders. Let your hands bring healing, soothing, feelings, full of caring.
  II. If participants are slightly uncomfortable, and discharge through laughing or chatting, facilitator reminds them to let their hands do their talking. Facilitator may help relax group by saying something like: "This is how all meetings of the United States Senate ought to begin." (Or, in an intact group, this is how all meetings of our group, faculty, staff, etc. should begin).
 III. This should last for three or four minutes. Facilitator then tells group to slowly let their hands come to rest and hold them on their neighbor's back for a minute in silent rest. Then slowly, very slowly, remove them, so gradually that the person doesn't realize they are gone.
 IV. Now turn around and massage the person who massaged you. Give your neighbor a comforting, soothing, caring massage the same way he massaged you. Try out on him some of the things he likes and things you like. After three or four minutes, the facilitator gives the same instructions about coming to a halt, very slowly and gradually, and after a minute or so, gently remove their hands.
  V. Volunteers may share in the large group how this felt, particularly how it affected their self-esteem and other feelings about self.
 VI. Group may brainstorm a list of persons or situations in which massage techniques can be used in personal and professional life to improve the esteem of those around us.
Variations
   I. Other types of massage can be used, such as back rub while lying on the floor, temple rubs, and arm massages, when the trust level has increased and group cohesiveness has grown.

Reference

Sidney B. Simon, "Please Touch! How to Combat Skin Hunger in Our Schools," **Scholastic Teacher,** October, 1974, pp. 22-25.

Sidney B. Simon, **Caring, Feeling, Touching** (Niles, Ill.: Argus Communications, 1976).

THE CAR WASH: Receiving Group Affection
Goals
    I. To experience group affection
    II. To give a lift to a "down" member
    III. To experience heightened self-esteem through group validation
Group Size
At least twelve or more participants
Time Required
Ten to twenty minutes
Materials
No special materials required
Physical Setting
Room large enough to have group stand in rows
Process
    I. Group members are divided into two, making parallel lines, standing close together.
    II. One member walks through the two lines and as he does so group members express verbal and nonverbal affection, appreciation and validation.
    III. Person who was "washed" should now be sparkling, shiny, cheery, happy, and bright. He may want to share his feelings after the experience with the group.
    IV. One or two members may want to experience the Car Wash each session of a training event, rather than have everyone do it at the same time. The spontaneity and enjoyment may remain more fresh that way. Or, all group members may go through the Car Wash on the same occasion, perhaps as a closure exercise.
Variations
    I. This exercise may also be used as a community builder and/or trust builder; or, alternatively, as a closure experience.
    II. Member who was "washed" may wish to comment further on his experiences, talking in greater depth about high points in his life when he felt "washed" and "sparkling" like now. Car Wash experience may help participants recall previous similar experiences, helping them become more in touch with other times when they received widespread affection and validation.

Adapted from Jack Canfield and Harold C. Wells, **100 Ways to Enhance Self Concept in the Classroom.** (Englewood Cliffs, N.J.: Prentice-Hall, 1976), p. 223.

BODY LIFT

Goals
    I. To experience group affection
    II. To learn to take in esteem and affection of others
    III. To let oneself be nourished by group and note effect on self-esteem

Group Size
    At least ten people

Time Required
    Ten minutes or more

Materials
    No special materials required

Physical Setting
    Room preferably with soft carpet for participant to lie on

Process
    I. A group member is selected to lie on the floor flat on his back with eyes closed.
    II. Group surrounds member and slowly and gently lifts him straight up in the air about waist high. Group may gently rock him and/or sing or hum softly to him.
    III. After a few minutes at this level, raise person up to neck level of those lifting him.
    IV. Gently and slowly lower participant to ground and tell him when he's ready he may get up.
    V. Lifted person may then comment on feelings and thoughts while experiencing the group lift.

Variations
    I. This exercise can be used effectively after a group member has experienced a "heavy" time of self-disclosure or other emotion-laded sharing or inter-relating. It rarely fails to create a deep sense of self-acceptance and warmth. Sensitive facilitators will watch out for creative opportunities to utilize this exciting experience.

CARING LIFT

Goals
    I. To experience the love, caring and affection of the group
    II. To experience the connection between others' caring and one's self-esteem
    III. To increase the affection level and trust level of the group
    IV. To increase the trust and affection level of two particular individuals
    V. To experience one's ability to totally let go and give oneself to the care of another person, and to receive love and caring.

Group Size
Can be done by one dyad or by many dyads simultaneously. No limit to number of dyads.

Time Required
Twenty to thirty minutes

Materials
None

Physical Setting
A room large enough for participants to lie flat on floor with dyadic partner having enough space to move around person on floor. Carpeted floor much preferred.

Process
    I. One person lies on floor, completely relaxed. Arms and legs unfolded, eyes closed. Let all tension flow out of the body.
    II. Dyadic partner places his hands gently on ankles of focus person. This is not a massage (which is a different experience altogether). Therefore dyadic partner does not rub or glide hands along body of focus person lying on floor. Rather dyadic partner will gently and slowly move his hands underneath one ankle of focus person and very slowly lift it as far as it can go comfortably without any stress. Slowly and gently lower it to floor. Success of this experience lies in ability of dyadic partner to lift and lower the leg very slowly with focus person letting dyadic partner do all the work while his own muscles are completely relaxed. Focus person will get feeling that he is letting himself go, and putting himself totally in the control and care of another.
    III. Repeat same caring lift with other body extremities: other leg, both arms, and head.
    IV. Focus person should lie still after exercise until ready to get up. He should rise only when feeling comfortable to do so, and then very slowly to avoid dizziness and possible fall from lack of balance. It is best to sit up first, then stand up.
    V. Focus person may then want to give his reactions to the experience. Some of these may be answers to these questions:
        1) How did it feel to experience love and care?
        2) Was he able to let go and trust his partner?
        3) What was the feeling of being totally in the care of another person?

    4) What effect did this experience have on his self-esteem?

    5) What implications are there for raising the self-esteem of significant persons in his life?

VI. Focus person and dyadic partner may now reverse roles, with dyadic partner receiving the "caring lift."

Variations

I. In addition to the **arms, legs and head-neck,** one may also want to place hands under **lower back and lift** the person's back in the air a few inches. This **should be done** with caution since many people have lower-back problems and might experience pain. Also, it takes a very strong person to be able to do this slowly and carefully.

I learned this experience from the Rev. Bob Jacoby of Springfield, Pa.

GROUP APPLAUSE: Experiencing Group Esteem
Goals
   I. To have participants experience feelings of group esteem and affection
  II. To help a person who may be feeling momentary self-esteem
 III. To help a person who came late or feels outside the group
 IV. To help participants examine their need for and appreciation of group esteem. To feel effect of group esteem on self-esteem
  V. To help members learn names and appearances of other group members
Group Size
Ten or more people
Time Required
About 60 seconds for each participant, or at least ten minutes
Materials
   none
Physical Setting
Enough room for group to sit in circle and have participant go in center

Process
   I. **In early stage of group formation, before members know each other,** each person in group takes a turn being focus person, going into center of group. Focus person says: "My name is...." Group applauds and cheers loudly for full sixty seconds. Focus person may acknowledge applause any way he wishes.
  II. Have all members of group take turns being focus person before discussion of feelings of other reactions.
 III. When entire group has finished, individuals may discuss their own reactions or give feedback to others regarding their reactions and appearance.
Variation
   I. Same exercise may be done as closure, but care should be taken to see that this does not turn into an applause contest with those getting a lot of applause experiencing approval by group, and others getting low applause experiencing rejection. Thus, this exercise works best at early stages of group formation. Car wash is similar strategy for later or final stages of the group.
  II. Group may want to discuss issue of artificiality and spontaneity. How did it feel praising a person, affirming a person you don't know? (Groups usually find this a pleasant and useful exercise despite surface feelings of artificiality.) Do we all have a need to love and reach out to others, even if we don't know them? And to receive love from strangers?)
 III. Group may want to discuss what thoughts and images they had of focus persons as they were applauding and cheering them. This can be useful for further positive feedback.
Adapted from Erving & Miriam Polster, **Gestalt Therapy Integrated** (N.Y.: Vintage Books, Random House, 1974), p. 305.

NONVERBAL FEEDBACK: A Group Validation Exercise

Goals
  I. To help participants feel affection and validation of the group
  II. To create a climate of group affection and intimacy

Group Size
  Ten or more preferably

Time Required
  Ten to fifteen minutes

Materials
  None

Physical Setting
  No special requirements

Process
  I. At intervals during the course of the life of a group, either a one-session or multi-session workshop, one volunteer may come forward and become focus person. Facilitator sends focus person into center of circle, and tells him to close his eyes.
  II. The group is then told, "Whoever so desires may now approach X and express affection and validation nonverbally in any way you wish." After a few minutes, members return to the circle.
  III. Focus person describes his feelings while receiving nonverbal positive feedback.

Variation
  I. If one particular person in the group is feeling excluded or in a low mood, or has received negative feedback that upset him, facilitator can suggest that he come into the center of the circle and become the focus person in this exercise.

Chapter 7

SELF-ESTEEM FOR MINORITY GROUPS

If individuals can be adversely affected by put-downs and derisive, humiliating attitudes, behaviors and remarks of others, what about groups, social units? Can they experience the same lack of self-esteem which a person does under similar circumstances and begin to manifest the resultant neurotic, defensive and insecure behavior?

According to several authorities, and according to my own personal observations and experience, the answer is Yes. William Schutz attests that "the laws that hold for man as a unified organism **also apply to a group and large social units** (emphasis added). The principles used to understand individuals and groups are, in essence, the same." [1] Purkey reports a study that "shows that not only is there a connection between the self concept and behavior, but that in pre-school and young school children there is awareness of racial and religious group membership which contributes an abasing or enhancing quality to the child's self concept." [2]

What is the process of forming low self-esteem among such religious, racial, and ethnic groups? The same as it is in an individual. A young child, for example, whose parents treat him and speak to him as if he were unworthy and useless, begins to **internalize** the opinion of his parents and to look upon himself as unworthy and useless. With a larger social unit the same process takes place. The member of such a group internalizes what is said about his **group** as applying to himself. If Blacks, Jews, Indians, Chicanos, women, are less human than white Anglo-Saxon Protestant males, in the eyes of the majority population, then many, if not most, members of the Black, Jewish, Indian, Chicano, and female minorities [3] at some time in their lives accept at least part of the opinion that the majority culture holds for all members of their religious, racial or other group. Kenneth B. Clark says that "Children who are consistently rejected understandably begin to question and doubt whether they, their family, and their group really deserve no more respect from the larger society than they receive." [4]

When such children grow up, after experiencing prejudice and discrimination throughout their early years, they begin to act in ways that demonstrate their low self concept. Joseph Stein describes the unfortunate effects this syndrome has on the personality of such a minority group member: [5]

Many members of ethnic minorities have taken a defensive approach to relations with other group. Their most characteristic reactions to prejudice have been denying their membership in a minority group, withdrawing from other groups, striving to compensate for their membership in a minority, becoming prejudiced themselves, or fighting back against the majority.

The person who is insecure as a member of an ethnic minority tends to accept the majority's negative perception of him. His self-esteem is poor, and he sees himself as less worthy than members of the more privileged groups. He may insist that he is as good as they are, but he does not really believe it. In subtle ways, and despite himself, he imparts this conviction of inferiority to his children as he rears them. As he unconsciously identifies with the majority point of view, he is guilty of prejudice against himself and his own people. If he is a light-complected black, he may try to "pass" as white. Unfortunately, in repudiating himself and his background, his personality is undermined so that he remains unintegrated in any group.

The process of internalizing the hatred and prejudice of the majority culture has the effect of making the object of such hate and prejudice his own worst enemy. The prejudiced individual has unwittingly drawn his victim into becoming his ally and punishing himself even more than an outsider could. What we then have is what S. I. Hayakawa calls "the most insidious form of Jim Crow," or "Jim Crow of the mind." [6] He writes: "Physical Jim Crow is imposed by others—by fences, barricades, 'white' and 'colored' signs over drinking fountains. But Jim Crow of the mind is not that which is enforced by headwaiters, employment agencies, railroad companies, or the police....Long after a national fair-employment-practices law is on the books, long after the last segregated schoolhouse in the United States is abolished, we shall still have to reckon with Jim Crow of the mind...."

The member of a minority group who internalizes the blind hatred and viscious attacks of the majority group in society not only does a disservice to his own culture and to the majority culture, but can lead a life of misery, alienation and emotional instability.

Milton Steinberg quotes several opinions regarding the effects of such self-hatred on Jews. [7] "...writing in **The Menorah Journal** of the summer. of 1942, Professor Salo Baron asserts: 'There are in all western Jewish communities innumerable Jews whom I have frequently ventured to style the "inverted Marranos." Those appear and act outwardly as Jews; they are recognized as Jews by themselves and their environment. But they deeply resent this fact which, for one reason or another, they cannot alter. Such inverted Marranos, hating their Jewish heritage and involuntary allegiance, usually become self-haters of a pathological kind. They not only destroy their own peace of mind; they are a menace to the equilibrium of the general as well as Jewish society around them.'"

Steinberg, in the same passage, quotes social psychologist Kurt Lewin, who, writing in **The Contemporary Jewish Record**, June, 1941, said: "That self-hatred is present among Jews is a fact that the non-Jew would hardly believe, but which is well known among Jews themselves."

Jewish sociologist Manheim Shapiro also testifies in a study he did, to wide-spread Jewish self-hatred: [8]

When we ask our respondents if they are ever embarrassed by the behavior of other Jews, a majority says "yes." When they are asked to describe the kinds of behavior which embarrass them, it turns out to be the whole catalogue of charges leveled at the whole group of Jews by anti-Semites: "loud, noisy, vulgar, pushing, clannish, money-minded." Of course, it is always **other Jews** who are guilty of this behavior. But does this not reflect something in the consciousness or subconscious of those who are giving the answer? Does not even the claimed embarrassment of the behavior of **other** Jews reflect a hyper-sensitivity that suggests an uneasiness with the group identification?

The question can well be asked, Does this internalization of the prejudice of the majority culture towards minorities affect only the faint-hearted and the insecure? Only those whose families and communities who do not instill a more positive self-acceptance and self-pride into them? To an extent, that is true. But when the majority view is widespread, as racism, anti-Semitism, and other dangerous forms of group hatred, even the most self-accepting families and individuals are infected by the germ of self-hatred.

Nathan Wright, Jr., a Black activist scholar, describes the process of self-hatred that took place in his family even though his parents had a healthy sense of pride in their Negro heritage: [9]

> Our parents were eager that we come to see ourselves in a positive way and to accept our heritage as good. Yet somehow I came to feel that although my mother's rich golden-brown complexion was the most beautiful that God had made, it was still necessary to improve upon His work. Thick lips, for instance, had to be kept pulled in tight lest they appear too large.
>
> Mom, like many other mothers of that period, would have us stand before a mirror and go through the exercise of saying "prunes and prisms" while pulling our lips in gently. Madam A'Lelia Walker, who invented the hot hair-straightening comb, was also a kind of patron saint in our household. Our parents dressed us somewhat lavishly. We were scrubbed and brushed and pressed, and our arms and legs were oiled so that the ashen or rusty look that dark skin often develops in cold weather would take on a satiny luster. We were taught to be proud but also to be as much like the white ideal as our black selves could be. Like so many "refined" white Americans who try to emulate the English, we either could not or would not accept ourselves for what we were. We were not even conscious of our self-depreciation....
>
> Unconscious black self-hatred is the black side of the racism that permeates the nation. It is self-destructive insofar as it works to make black people "acceptable" and worthwhile to the larger society at the price of diminishing black identity, integrity and self-respect.

The insidious effects of majority prejudice on young children are more far-reaching than the average person realizes. In my own case, I know that there was a fierce pride and delight in living as a Jew in my primary family. However, from time to time I find myself being embarrassed at other "pushy" Jews, or when a Jew is involved in a public crime, such as Jack Ruby, who assassinated President Kennedy's assassin, Lee Harvey Oswald. I frequently find myself searching for Jewish-sounding names in news articles, hoping not to be embarrassed by a Rabbi Baruch Korff, or a Rabbi Meir Kahane, who might "besmirch the Jewish name."

Cynthia N. Shepard, Associate Professor of Education at Texas Southern University, a Black scholar and author, describes the adverse effects of American racism on her young son, Mark, in a piece called "The World Through Mark's Eyes." [10]

I would like you to know my son Mark, who is now five years old. Although he has not yet attended kindergarten, he can both read and write, and can accurately identify colors and forms with an acuity beyond his years. He collects American flags and pictures and ceramics of our national emblem, the eagle. He learned from somewhere on his own initiative the Pledge of Allegiance, which he recites with deep fervor. He only asked me the definitions of those difficult words: **indivisible, liberty, justice.** My precious, precocious Mark is proud of his white, Anglo-Saxon heritage. But, he's black: a beautifully carved and polished piece of black American earth.

You may debate with me whether I should have taught him from birth that he is black. Instead, I invite you to see the world through Mark's eyes. Mark learned to read when he was three years old—books based on the white American style of life with pictures of blond, blue-eyed suburbia, with decent interspersing of browns and brunets—but no blacks. He watched the "educational" newsreels on television, which for him reinforced the rightness of whiteness. The man in the white hat—beating the black man with a billy club and then kicking him into insensibility—was the good guy. He was the proctor of our individual rights. The books said so.

Black is the night which Mark fears, vanquished by the white of day. White is the knight on the white horse charging the black stains of daily living, and they all vanish. Black is unwanted; black is weak and easily defeated; black is bad.

I took Mark South with me and I placed him in an all-black nursery school while I taught during the day. The first evening, when I brought him home, he was in tears, writhing and retching in painful confusion. "Why did you make me go to school with all those Negroes?"

Then, just like NOW, I dig! Intellectuality had blocked my insight, creating of me a blind broad and of my black son a white racist. In his innocence—or highest sophistry, you see—he had intuitively perceived race not as a color, but as an attitude that he did not exemplify. My arguments to the contrary were completely hushed by his own words: "You said I could be anything I choose, and I choose to be white."

Of course, the solution to this problem of lack of self-esteem among minority group members is to eradicate racism, religionism, sexism, male chauvinism, and every other "ism" from society. However, until that becomes the prevailing situation, those who seem to do best are those who joyously accept their heritage, accept membership in their group, and do not try to "pass" or assimilate or deny their origins or heritage. Elie Wiesel writes: "To realize himself, the Baal Shem's Hasidism teaches us, man must first of all remain faithful to his most intimate, truest self; he cannot help others if he negates himself....A Jew who rejects his origins, his brothers, to make a so-called contribution to mankind, will in the end betray mankind. That is true for all men." [11]

Congressperson Shirley Chisholm made the same observation in a speech to the student body of Federal City College, Washington, D.C., when she stated that "Black people have freed themselves from the dead weight of the albatross of blackness that once hung about their neck. They have done it by picking it up in their arms and holding it out with pride for all the world to see. They have done it by embracing it—not in the dark moon, but in the searing light of the white sun. They have said 'Yes' to it and found that the skin that was once seen as symbolizing their shame is in reality their badge of honor." [12]

Saul Teplitz's parable of the scottie dog who finally accepted who he really was is a beautiful summary of the point of this chapter, namely, that self-acceptance is crucial to personality health, and that self-acceptance entails being comfortable with, and, even more significantly, celebrating, who one is, including his minority group status: [13]

There was once a scottie dog who found himself lost and alone in a neighborhood of Irish terriers. Every time the scottie walked down the street, the terriors would bark at him in rage. He was quite puzzled and hurt, but instead of wondering what bothered the terriers, he began to analyze himself. Perhaps the terriers barked at him because he was different. He, therefore, tried very hard to be like the terriers. He began to wag his tail as they did and to prick up his ears as they did. He even barked in as perfect an imitation as could be achieved. And still they barked every time he went by.

The scottie then decided to call in experts to write scholarly dissertations which would prove the greatness of the contributions of the scotties to canine civilization. Soon there were mountains of statistics to point up the courage of the scotties through a computation of the number of people they had rescued from burning buildings and drownings. Unfortunately, the only ones that read the books and the statistics were other scotties. Whatever the scottie did to impress or to imitate left the terriers unmoved. They continued to bark as in the past. Finally, the scottie decided that since he was a scottie, he had better act like one and live like one, and be the best possible scottie he could be. And if the terriers still barked, there was nothing he could do about it.

135

FOOTNOTES

1. **Here Comes Everybody** (N.Y.: Harrow Books, Harper & Row, 1972), p. xviii.
2. William W. Purkey, **Self Concept and School Achievement** (Englewood Cliffs, N.J.: Prentice-Hall, 1970), p. 38.
3. Women are, of course, approximately 50% of the population but view themselves sociologically as an oppressed group, if not in numbers then in power.
4. **Dark Ghetto** (N.Y.: Harper and Row, 1965), p. 63.
5. **Effective Personality: A Humanistic Approach** (Belmont, Ca.: Brooks/Cole, 1972), p. 175.
6. **Symbols, Status, and Personality** (N.Y.: Harcourt, Brace and World, 1963), pp. 82-3.
7. Milton Steinberg, **A Partisan Guide to the Jewish Problem** (N.Y.: Bobbs-Merrill, 1945), p. 115.
8. "Changing Jewish Attitudes," **Journal of Jewish Communal Service,** Volume 37, Summer, 1961, p. 407.
9. **Let's Work Together** (N.Y.: Hawthorn, 1968), pp. 119-121.
10. James A. Banks and Jean D. Grambs, eds., **Black Self-Concept: Implications for Education and Social Science** (N.Y.: McGraw-Hill 1972), pp. 1-3.
11. **Souls on Fire** (N.Y.: Random House, 1972), p. 32.
12. Quoted in Arthur C. Littelton and Mary W. Burger, eds., **Black Viewpoints** (N.Y.: A Mentor Book, 1971), p. 348.
13. **Life Is For Living** (N.Y.: Jonathan David, 1969), pp. 66-67.

Chapter 8

CURRICULAR MATERIALS ON BUILDING SELF-ESTEEM

In the past ten years the importance of the student's self concept in learning has received wider recognition. Research studies and other writings, such as those of Stanley Coopersmith, William Purkey, Arthur Combs, Don E. Hamachek, Jack Canfield and others have generated an interest on the part of students, teachers, educators, librarians and publishers to produce more and more school materials to help raise the self-esteem of learners as a prior condition to effective learning.

Listed below are some of the materials designed for classroom and family use, as well as for individual and personal growth.

I. School Curriculum Materials

1. **100 Ways to Enhance Self-Concept in the Classroom,** by Jack Canfield and Harold Wells. Englewood Cliffs, N.Y.: Prentice-Hall, Inc. Paperback edition, $6.95. This is the single best book for teachers who want to introduce into their classrooms activities to help their students appreciate who they are and accept themselves for what they are. It contains excellent activities, a brief but highly useful theoretical introduction, and an excellent list of resources in the back. Jack Canfield offers superb workshops on self-concept enhancement and other areas of humanistic and transpersonal education through the Center for Wholistic Education, Box 575, Amherst, MA 01102.

2. **About Me: A Curriculum for a Developing Self,** by Harold Wells and John T. Canfield (the same person who co-authored the book above, but who now uses the name "Jack" instead of "John"). Encyclopedia Britannica Education Corporation, 425 N. Michigan Ave., Chicago, Illinois 60611. There is a Student Book for 69 cents and Teacher's guide for $3.95. One of the best available curriculum materials on self concept. There are 17 lessons, each of which has several activities from which the teacher can choose or adapt. It is designed for grade 4 through 6. The first lesson, "I Work Better When I Am Comfortable in the Group," provides getting acquainted activities. Others are: "I Know Who I Am," "I Know My Strengths," "I Can Set and Achieve Goals," "I Try to Be Myself," and "I Am in Charge of Becoming Myself."

3. "Humanistic and Transpersonal Education: A Guide to Resources" by Jack Canfield, in **The 1978 Annual Handbook for Group Facilitators,** Ed. J. Wm. Pfeiffer and John E. Jones (La Jolla: University Associates, 1978), pp. 277-292. A marvelous annotated bibliography, many of whose inclusions relate directly and indirectly to self concept.

4. **The IALAC Story,** by Sidney B. Simon. This is a story of a young student who wakes up in the morning feeling good about himself (I Am Loveable And Capable). However, after proceeding through family difficulties, put-downs in school by teacher and friends, little pieces of his IALAC (I am Loveable and Capable) sign are torn away until almost nothing is left. It has the added charm of being funny and entertaining as well as highly informative. There is a colorful booklet available at 50 cents each in quantity, and a filmstrip of 81 frames, taking 8 minutes, for Jr. and Sr. High students, accompanied by cassette or record. Either the cassette or the record with the filmstrip are available from Argus Communications, 7440 Natchez Ave., Niles, Ill. 60648, at $20.

5. The Human Development Program, by Uvaldo Palomares, Geraldine Ball, and Harold Bessell. This is the "Magic Circle" program, designed to create opportunities for students to grow in the realm of feelings and emotions. It uses the vehicle of small group discussions, daily or weekly, to encourage personal awareness, confidence in self-competence and effective social interaction. Materials are available from the Human DEvelopment Training Institute, 7574 University Avenue, La Mesa, Ca. 92041.

6. **Strategies in Humanistic Education,** A multi-volume series by Tim Timmerman and Jim Ballard. Mandala, P.O. Box 796, Amherst, Mass. 01002. Mandala is a publishing and consulting firm in humanistic education, which published materials for the Magic Circle Program (see Item #4 in this list, above), as well as other materials. Perusal of their large catalog will help teachers and other helpers find useful materials on self-concept. On pages 61-71 of **Strategies** are ideas for raising self-esteem, such as "Circletime Topics," "Journal Entries," "Self-concept Inventory," "Creative Writing Titles," and others.

7. **The Green Circle Program.** This program is designed to help children accept people of different racial, ethnic and religious backgrounds, by recognizing and accepting their own uniqueness as human beings. The Green Circle is a symbol of the child's world, family, friends, neighbors and others. By learning how to accept differences in himself, in wealth, ethnicity, race, religion, size, sex and age, he comes to learn to accept each human being as a unique member of the human family. The program is designed for elementary school children and uses discussion, filmstrips, arts and crafts and games. It has been in use for twenty years. Books and other materials are available from Green Circle Program, Inc., 801 Market St., Phila., Pa. 19105.

8. **Achievement Competence Training,** by Russell A. Hill et al. ACT is

a comprehensive learning package which helps students set and achieve goals. This is an excellent program to help participants' motivation, self-confidence and self-realization. Available from Research for Better Schools, 1700 Market St., Suite 1700, Phila., Pa. 19103.

9. **Achievement Motivation Materials,** by Alfred Alschuler, Diane Tabor and James McIntyre. A curriculum program for ninth graders, adapted from the achievement Motivation Development Project at Harvard University. Available from Education Ventures, Inc., 209 Court St., Middletown, CT. 06457.

10. **Developing Understanding of Self and Others** (DUSO) by Don Dinkmeyer. A program to help elementary school children understand themselves and those around them. Available from American Guidance Service, Inc., Dept. EL-4, Publishers' Building, Circle Pines, Minn. 55014.

11. **Dimensions of Personality Series,** by Walter J. Limbacher. Dayton, Ohio: George A. Pflaum. A series of books for children of different ages designed to be experiential and discussion-centered, built around well-selected readings on each level.

12. **Focus on Self Development,** by Judith L. Anderson, Carole J. Lang, and Virginia R. Scott. An affective educational program for children grades one to three, guided toward an understanding of self, others and environment, including filmstrips, records, photoboards, pupil activity books and teacher's guide. Available from Science Research Associates, 259 E. Erie St., Chicago, Ill. 60611.

13. **I Have Feelings,** by Terry Berger. For children ages 4 to 9, this book deals with seventeen different feelings, including good and bad ones, and the situations that brought them about. Available from Behavioral Publications, 2852 Broadway, New York, N.Y. 10025.

14. **Motivation Advance Program,** by Audrey J. Peterson. An experiential program to help junior high and high school students expand their views of self-acceptance and see themselves as worthy and unique individuals. It includes topics such as community building, achievement patterns, developing human potential, value clarification, goal setting and conflict management. Available from Achievement Motivation System, 111 E. Wacker Drive, Chicago, Ill. 60601.

15. **Self-Enhancing Education:** A Program to Motivate Learners, by Norma Randolph and William Howe. Palo Alto: Educational Progress Corp., 1966. A teacher's handbook describing ideas for teachers to use in helping students raise self-esteem. Available from Self-Enhancing

Education, Inc. (S.E.E., Inc.), 1957 Pruneridge Avenue, Santa Clara, Ca. 95050.

16. **Study Guide for Building Self-Esteem and Home Study Course for Building Self-Esteem,** by I. S. Barksdale. Mr. Barksdale is a former industrialist who disposed of his worldwide business interests in 1964 to devote his life to establishing a Foundation for producing booklets, tapes, and articles, and organizing lectures, seminars, workshops and self-led study groups on self-esteem. The publicity brochure states that "The work and research of the (Barksdale) Foundation has confirmed lack of Self-Esteem to be the **major cause** of practically all emotional turmoil in the home—both of divorce and parent-offspring alienation and estrangement—of alcoholism, drug addiction, destructive competition, aggression, and practically all other emotional suffering and unhappiness...." Pamphlets, booklets, cassettes, and other materials for the Barksdale programs are available from The Barksdale Foundation, P.O. Box 187, Idyllwide, Ca. 92349.

17. **Teacher Effectiveness Training,** by Thomas Gordon. N.Y.: Peter H. Wyden, 1974. $9.95. The Gordon method, based on Carl Rogers' active listening through reflection of feeling and content, is a sound an useful method for helping students achieve high self-esteem. Gordon's organization, Effectiveness Training, Inc., runs trainers' workshops throughout the country to enable educators and others to give T.E.T. courses in local communities. For a list of courses in Teacher Effectiveness, Parent Effectiveness, Leader Effectiveness, Human Effectiveness, School Administrators Effectiveness, write Effectiveness Training, Inc., 531 Stevens Ave., Solana Beach, Ca. 92075.

18. **Peer Program for Youth,** by Ardyth Hebeisen. Minneapolis, Minn.: Augsburg Publishing House, 1973. This is an excellent handbook of experiential activities and discussion topics related to self-esteem, self-understanding and communication skills. The word "Peer" in the title is an acronym for "Positive Educational Experiences in Relationships." Workshops on the PEER program are offered by Ardyth Hebeisen and Barbara Glaser-Kirschenbaum at the National Humanistic Education Center, 110 Spring St., Saratoga Springs, N.Y. 12866. NHEC has a large catalog of workshops and books on humanistic education, many of which deal with various aspects of self-esteem and self-awareness.

19. **Reaching Out,** by David W. Johnson. Englewood Cliffs, N.J.: Prentice-Hall, Inc., 1972. An excellent book of experience-based learning programs on interpersonal effectiveness and self-actualization, including chapters on "Self-Disclosure" and "Acceptance of Self and Others." High school age range.

20. **Free to Be...You and Me,** ed. Francine Klagsbrun with forward by Marlo Thomas. N.Y.: Webster Division, McGraw-Hill Book Co., 1974. A popular book and record dealing with self-acceptance and self-esteem, for adults and children.

21. **Glad To Be Me: Building Self-Esteem in Yourself and Others,** ed. Dov Peretz Elkins. Englewood Cliffs, N.Y.: Prentice-Hall, 1976. This is an anthology of brief selections, divided into sixteen chapters, including themes on self-acceptance, self-trust, self-affirmation, self-love, avoiding put-downs, self image, raising self-esteem in children and students, and loving your body. There are beautiful photographs accompanying the text. Since I edited the book, I really love it!

22. **God Made Me—I'm Glad,** by Dorothy L. Dysard. Phila.: Westminster Press, 1976. This is a program designed for church school, kindergartners, including a student's book (95 cents), Leader's Guide ($2.25), and Resource Packet ($6.75) of record, game, poster, and pictures. Other materials in this series are available from Cooperative Publication Association (CPA), Box 179, St. Louis, Mo. 63166.

23. **Jump to Learn: Teaching Motor Skills for Self-Esteem,** by Lida Colwell. A detailed 12-week lesson plan to help children feel comfortable with themselves before beginning new learning in school—i.e., for pre-school and kindergarten children. The kit contains a teacher's guidebook and ten individualized booklets, for $12.95. Available from Pennant Educational Materials, 4680 Alvarado Cyn. Rd. San Diego, Ca. 92120.

24. **People Projects,** by Merrill Harmin. Materials for students in grades 4 through 8, to help deal with values, feelings, imagination, and problem-solving. One unit is devoted solely to self concept, but others are related closely to it. Each set of 120 large, color activity cards, costs $19.92, and is available from Addison Wesley Publishing Co., Sand Hill Rd., Menlo Park, Ca. 94025.

25. **Claude.** An excellent, three-minute colored film, produced in 1969, about a little boy whose parents constantly put him down and whose inventive potential must be realized through his own efforts. This cartoon film makes an excellent point, is humorous, and extremely effective. Available for purchase for $80 through Pyramid Film Distributors, Box 1048, Santa Monica, Ca. 90406. It may be available for rental through a local school or library.

25. **Transactional Analysis.** There are several books and booklets based on Eric Berne's method of Transactional Analysis. Alvyn M.

Freed has written **T.A. For Kids and Grown Ups Too,** \$4., and **T.A. For Tots and Other Prinzes,** \$5.95. These are available from Jalmar Press, 391 Monroe St., Sacramento, Ca. 95815. These books stress the importance of saying and feeling, "I'm OK, You're OK." A Jr. High and Sr. High text for a course on T.A. is found in **Am I OK?** by Paul L. Philllips and Franklin D. Cordell, available at \$4.95 from Argus Communications, 7400 Natchez Ave., Niles, Ill. 60648. Available together with the book is a set of 30 spirit masters for \$15. and a set of 26 TA posters for \$17.50. The entire kit of book, spirit masters and posters are available for \$34.

27. **Guidance Associates** filmstrips and cassettes. Three sets of 2 filmstrips and accompanying LP record of cassette are available for \$48 per set frm Buidance Associates, 757 Third Avenue, New York, N.Y. 10017. The first is "Reflections of Myself," including poetry, prose and photos by high school students dealing with self-acceptance and self-affirmation. Another is "Hard to Feel You're Somebody: Dope in the City,"—frank and powerful comments by youngsters from the inner city exploring relationships between the grinding pressures of daily life, peer norms, seeming irrelevance of school, and drug use. It shows ways individuals have kicked drugs through personal relationships, rebuilt self-image, and involvement with religion and social action. The third is "Everything But...," with Professor Richard Hettlinger of Kenyon College discussing the characteristics and importance of self-respect as expressed socially, sexually, ethically and emphasizing fidelity to one's own feelings.

28. **Self-Concept Sourcebook,** ed. Dov Peretz Elkins. This is an anthology of some of the best theoretical and practical writings on self-concept enhancement available, including selections by Rogers, Maslow, Fromm, Fitts, Purkey, Canfield, and many other leading humanistic thinkers. It is designed as a college text, but can be used for many other purposes such as in-service training, adult study groups and individual reading. Available from Growth Associates, Box 8429, Rochester, N.Y. 14618.

29. **Building Positive Self-Concepts in Children: Ideas for Teachers,** by Donald W. Felker. Purdue University, Child Development & Family Life, 1974. An excellent 158-page collection of practical ideas for teachers.

II. Reading Books for Children Which Help Improve Self Concept

A. Books for the Young Reader (Pre-school through third grade)

Buckley, Helen E. **Michael Is Brave.** N.Y.: Lothrop, 1971

Conford, Ellen. **Just the Thing for Geraldine.** Boston: Little Brown, 1974.

Hodges, Elizabeth. **Free As a Frog.** Reading, Mass.: Addison-Wesley, 1969.

Hopkins, Lee Bennett. **Me!** N.Y.: Seabury, 1970.

Klein, Norma. **Girls Can Be Anything.** N.Y.: Dutton, 1973.

Krasilovsky, Phyllis. **Very Little Boy.** Garden City, N.Y.: Doubleday, 1962.

—————. **Very Little Girl.** Garden City, N.Y.: Doubleday, 1953.

Kraus, Robert. **Leo the Late Bloomer.** N.Y.: Windmill, 1971.

Munro, Leaf. **Ferdinand.** N.Y.: Viking, 1963.

Palmer, Pat. **Liking Myself.** San Luis Obispo, Ca.: Impact Publishers, 1978.

Scott, Ann Herbert. **Sam.** N.Y.: McGraw Hill, 1967.

Sonneborn, Ruth A. **Lollipop Party.** N.Y.: Viking, 1967.

Stanley, John. **It's Nice to Be Little.** N.Y.: Rand McNally, 1969.

Stone, Elberta. **I'm Glad I'm Me.** N.Y.: Putnam, 1971.

B. Reading Books for the Intermediate Reader (4th through 6th grade)

Blume, Judy. **Are You There God, It's Me Margaret.** N.Y.: Bradbury, 1970.

—————. **Otherwise Known as Sheila the Great.** N.Y.: Dutton, 1972.

—————. **Tales of a Fourth Grade Nothing.** N.Y.: Dutton, 1972.

Conford, Ellen. **Dreams of Victory.** Boston: Little, Brown, 1973.

Cretan, Gladys. **All Except Sammy.** Boston: Little, Brown, 1966.

Kingman, Lee. **The Year of the Raccoon.** Boston: Houghton Mifflin, 1966.

Klein, Norma. **Taking Sides.** N.Y.: Pantheon, 1974.

Norris, Gunilla. **The Top Step.** N.Y.: Atheneum, 1970.

Palmer, Pat. **The Mouse, the Monster and Me!** San Luis Obispo, Ca.: Impact Publishers, 1978.

Shore, June. **What the Matter with Wakefield?** Nashville: Abingdon, 1974.

Stolz, Mary. **Bully of Barkham Street.** N.Y.: Harper, 1963.

C. Reading Books for the Upper Reader (6th through 8th grade)

Byars, Betsy. **Summer of the Swans.** N.Y.: Viking, 1970.

Grohskopf, Bernice. **Shadow in the Sun.** N.Y.: Atheneum, 1975.

Smith, Doris. **Tough Chauncey.** N.Y.: Morrow, 1974.

144

BIBLIOGRAPHY

A. SELF-ESTEEM

Allport, Gordon W. **The Person in Psychology**—Selected Essays. Boston: Beacon Press, 1968. "Psychological Models for Guidance," chapter 4, pp. 67-80.

Angyal, Andras. "A Theoretical Model for Personality Studies," **Journal of Personality,** Vol. 20, #1, September, 1951.

Ansbacher, Heinz L. and Rowena R. Ansbacker, eds. **The Individual Psychology of Alfred Adler:** A Systematic Presentation in Selections from His Writings. New York: Harper Torchbooks, 1967.

Assagioli, Roberto. **Psychosynthesis.** New York: The Viking Press, 1971.

Bach, George R. and Herbert Goldberg. **Creative Aggression**—The Art of Assertive Living. Garden City, New York: Doubleday, 1974.

Belgum, David R. **What Can I Do About the Part of Me I Don't Like?** Minneapolis, Minn.: Augsburg Publishing House, 1974.

Benjamins, James. "Changes in Relation to Influences Upon Self-Conceptualization," **Journal of Abnormal and Social Psychology.** 45:473-480, 1950.

Benson, Lou. **Images, Heroes and Self-Perceptions.** Englewood Cliffs, New Jersey: Prentice-Hall, 1974. Chapter 3, "The Put-Down," pp. 45-76.

Berger, Emanuel M. "The Relation Between Expressed Acceptance of Self and Expressed Acceptance of Others," **Journal of Abnormal and Social Psychology,** 47:778-782, 1972.

Bernhard, Yetta. **How To Be Somebody**—Open the Door to Personal Growth. Millbrae, Ca.: Celestial Arts, 1975.

Blume, Robert A. "How the Child Sees Himself May Relate to How the Teacher Sees Himself" **Michigan Education Journal.** 46:9-11, November, 1968.

Branden, Nathaniel. **The Psychology of Self Esteem.** New York: Bantam Books, 1971.

_____. **The Disowned Self.** New York: Bantam Books, 1973.

Briggs, Dorothy Corkille. **Your Child's Self-Esteem.** Garden City, New York: Doubleday, 1970.

Bryant, Gay and Bockris-Wylie. **How I Learned to Like Myself.** New York: Warner Paperback Library, 1975.

Buss, S. H. **Psychology: Man in Perspective.** New York: Wiley, 1973.

Butler, John M. and Gerard V. Haigh. "Changes in the Relation Between Self-concepts and Ideal Concepts Consequent Upon Client-Centered Counseling," in **Psychology and Personality Change,** ed. Carl R. Rogers and Rosalind F. Dymond. Chicago: University of Chicago Press, 1954, pp. 55-75.

Coleman James C. and Constance L. Hammen. **Contemporary Psychology and Effective Behavior.** Glenview, Ill.: Scott, Foresman & Co., 1974.

Combs, Arthur W., Donald L. Avila and William W. Purkey. **Helping Relationships**—Basic Concepts for the Helping Professions. Boston: Allyn and Bacon, 1971. Chapter 3, "Self-Concept: Product and Producer of Experience," pp. 39-61. Chapter 8, "Freedom and Self-Actualization," pp. 143-164.

Combs, Arthur W., "What Can Man Become?" In **The Helping Relationship Sourcebook,** Donald L. Avila, Arthur W. Combs, William W. Purkey, eds. Boston: Allyn and Bacon, 1971.

_____, ed. **Perceiving, Behaving, Becoming**—A New Focus for Education. Association for Supervision and Curriculum Development, NEA, 1201 Sixteenth St., N.W., Washington, D.C. 20036, 1962. Chapter 7, "Motivation and the Growth of Self," chapter 8, "The Positive View of Self," chapter 9, "Acceptance and the Accurate View of Self."

Coopersmith, Stanley. **The Antecedents of Self-Esteem.** San Francisco: W. H. Freeman & Co., 1967.

_____. "Studies in Self-Esteem." **Scientific American,** February, 1968, pp. 96-106.

Dobson, James. **Hide or Seek**—Self-Esteem for the Child. Old Tappan, New Jersey: Fleming H. Revell Co., 1974.

Elkins, Dov Peretz, ed. **Glad To Be Me**—**Building Self-Esteem in Yourself and Others.** Englewood Cliffs, New Jersey: Prentice-Hall, 1976.

_____. **Self-Concept Sourcebook.** Rochester, N.Y.: Growth Associates, 1978.

Evans, Richard I. **Carl Rogers**—The Man and His Ideas. New York: E. P. Dutton, 1975. Part II—Rogers' Conception of the Self, pp. 13-20.

Felker, Donald W. **Building Positive Self-Concepts.** Minneapolis, Minn.: Burgess Pub. Co., 1974.

Fensterheim, Herbert and Jean Baer. **Don't Say Yes When You Want to Say No**—How Assertiveness Training Can Change Your Life. New York: David McKay Company, Inc., 1975.

Fisher, Seymour. **Body Consciousness, You Are What You Feel.** Englewood Cliffs, New Jersey: Prentice-Hall, Inc., 1973.

Fitts, William H. and William T. Hamner. **The Self Concept and Delinquency.** Nashville, Tenn.: Counselor Recordings and Tests, 1969.

_____. **Interpersonal Competence: The Wheel Model.** Nashville, Tenn.: Counselor Recordings and Tests, 1970.

_____. **The Self Concept and Behavior: Overview and Supplement.** Nashville, Tenn.: Counselor Recordings and Tests, 1972.

_____. **The Self Concept and Performance.** Nashville, Tenn.: Counselor Recordings and Tests, 1972.

_____. **The Self Concept and Psychopathology.** Nashville, Tenn.: Counselor Recordings and Tests, 1972.

_____, et al. **The Self Concept and Self-Actualization.** Nashville, Tenn.: Counselor Recordings and Tests, 1971.

Frerichs, A. H. "Relationship of Self-Esteem of the Disadvantaged to School Success," **Journal of Negro Education,** 40:117-120, 1971.

Fromm, Erich. **The Art of Loving.** New York: Harper and Row, 1956.

_____. **Man for Himself.** "Selfishness, Self-Love, and Self-Interest." New York: Rinehart & Co., 1947, pp. 119-140.

Gilmore, John V. **The Productive Personality.** San Francisco: Albion Publishing Co., 1974.

Gilmore, John V. "Parent Counseling: Theory and Application," **Journal of Education,** Vol. 154, #1. October 1971, pp. 40-49.

_____. "Parental Counseling and Academic Achievement" **Journal of Education,** Vol. 149, #3, February 1967, pp. 46-69.

Ginott, Haim. **Between Parent and Child.** New York: Avon Books, 1969.

_____. **Between Parent and Teen-ager.** New York: Avon Books, 1971.

_____. **Teacher and Child.** New York: Avon Books. 1972.

Glasser, William. **Schools Without Failure.** New York: Harper and Row, 1969.

Gordon, Thomas. **Parent Effectiveness Training.** New York: Peter H. Wyden, Inc., Publisher, 1970.

_____. **Teacher Effectiveness Training.** New York: Peter H. Wyden, 1974.

Hamachek, Don E. **Encounters with the Self.** New York: Holt, Rinehart & Winston, 1971.

_____, ed. **The Self in Growth, Teaching and Learning.** Englewood Cliffs, New Jersey: Prentice-Hall, Inc., 1965.

_____. **Behavior Dynamics in Teaching, Learning and Growth.** Boston: Allyn and Bacon, 1975. Chapter 12, "Self-Concept Variables and Achievement Outcomes," pp. 532-579.

Harris, Thomas A. **I'm OK—You're OK.** New York: Harper and Row, 1967.

Hayakawa, S. I. **Symbol, Status and Personality.** New York: Harcourt Brace and World, 1963. Chapter 4, "The Self-Concept," pp. 36-50. Chapter 6, "The Self-Image and Intercultural Understanding, or How to Be Sane Though Negro," pp. 70-88.

Hebeisen, Ardyth. **Peer Program for Youth.** Minn.: Augsburg Press, 1973.

Horney, Karen. **Our Inner Conflicts.** New York: W. W. Norton and Co., Inc., 1945. Chapter 6, "The Idealized Image," pp. 96-114.

_____. **Neurosis and Human Growth.** New York: W. W. Norton and Co., Inc., 1950. Chapter 5, "Self-Hate and Self-Contempt," chapter 6, "Alienation from Self."

_____. **New Ways in Psychoanalysis.** New York: W. W. Norton and Co., Inc., 1939. Chapter 5, "The Concept of Narcissism," pp. 88-100.

Hulme, William. **When I Don't Like Myself**—A Youth Forum Book. New York: Thomas Nelson, Inc., 1971.

Jackins, Harvey. "The Complete Appreciation of Oneself." in **The Human Situation,** pp. 45-58. Seattle, Wash.: Rational Island Publishers, 1973.

James, William. **Psychology—The Briefer Course.** Edited by Gordon Allport. New York: Harper and Row, 1961. Chapter 3, "The Self," pp. 43-83.

Jersild, Arthur T. **When Teachers Face Themselves.** New York: Teachers College Press, Teachers College, Columbia University, 1955. Chapter 7.

_____. **In Search of Self.** An Exploration of the Role of the School in Promoting Self-Understanding. New York: Teachers College, Columbia University, 1952.

Johnson, David W. **Reaching Out—Interpersonal Effectiveness and Self-Actualization.** Englewood Cliffs, New Jersey: Prentice-Hall, 1972.

Jones, John E. "Assumptions about the Nature of Man." in 1972 **Annual Handbook for Group Facilitators,** J. William Pfeiffer and John E. Jones, eds. La Jolla, Ca.: University Associates, 1972.

Jourard, Sidney M. **Healthy Personality.** New York: Macmillan, 1974.

——————. **The Transparent Self,** 2nd ed. New York: D. Van Nostrand Co., 1971. pp. 38-41, 52-57.

Kolivosky, Michael E. and Laurence J. Taylor. **Why Do You See It That Way?** Hillsdale, Mich.: Kolivosky and Taylor, 1972.

LaBenne, William D. and Bert I. Greene. **Educational Implications of Self-Concept Theory.** Pacific Palisades, Ca.: Goodyear Publishing Co., 1969.

Laing, Ronald D. **Sanity, Madness and the Family.** Baltimore Md.: Penguin Books, 1970.

Lecky, Prescott. **Self-Consistency.** Garden City, New York: Doubleday, 1968.

Leviton, Charles D. **More Fully Human**—The Struggle to Be Me...With You. Costa Mesa, Ca.: Ronchuck Publishers (P.O. Box 1827), 1973. Chapter 2, "Do What's Best For You...Self Love, The Basis for Growth!" pp. 23-50.

Liebman, Joshua Loth. **Peace of Mind.** New York: Simon and Schuster, 1946. Chapter 3, "Love Thyself Properly," pp. 43-60.

Limbacher, Walter J. **Becoming Myself**—Dimensions of Personality. Dayton, Ohio: George Pflaum. Chapter 8, "I Don't Like Me," chapter 9, "If I Dislike Myself."

Lowry, Richard J. **Dominance, Self-Esteem, Self-Actulization: Germinal Papers of A. H. Maslow.** Monterey, Ca.: Brooks/Cole Publishing Co., 1973.

Maltz, Maxwell. **Creative Living For Today.** New York: Pocket Books, 1970.

——————. **Psycho-Cybernetics and Self-Fulfillment.** New York: Bantam Books, 1973. Chapter 6, "Self-Acceptance and Self-Fulfillment," pp. 95-112.

——————. **The Magic Power of Self-Image Psychology.** New York: Pocket Books, 1970.

Maslow, Abraham H. **Motivation and Personality,** 2nd ed. New York: Harper and Row, 1970.

May, Rollo. **Power and Innocence.** New York: W. W. Norton and Co., 1972. "Self-Affirmation," pp. 137-141. "Self-Assertion," pp. 142-146.

Mayeroff, Milton. **On Caring.** New York: Harper and Row, Perennial Library, 1971.

McDanald, Jr., Eugene C., Smith, Bert Kruger and Sutherland, Robert L. **Self-Acceptance.** (16-page pamphlet). Austin, Texas: Hogg Foundation for Mental Health, University of Texas, 1962.

McNeil, Elton B. **The Psychology of Being Human.** New York: Harper and Row, 1974. "Self-Esteem," pp. 105-7.

Meininger, Jut. **Success Through Transactional Analysis.** New York: New American Library, 1973.

Moustakas, Clark. **Individuality and Encounter.** Cambridge, Mass.: H. A. Doyle Publishing Co., 1968.

——————. **Personal Growth**—The Struggle for Identity and Human Values. Cambridge, Mass.: H. A. Doyle Publishing Co., 1969.

——————, ed. **The Self**—Explorations in Personal Growth. New York: Harper—Colophon Books, 1974. Chapter 1, "True Experience and the Self," Clark E. Moustakas, pp. 3-14.

Naranjo, Claudio. **The One Quest.** New York: Ballantine Books, 1973. "Self-acceptance," pp. 210-217.

Neisser, Edith G. **The Roots of Self-Confidence.** Chicago: Science Research Associates, Inc. 1970.

Newburger, Howard M. and Lee, Marjorie. **Winners and Losers: Self-Image Modification.** New York: David McKay Co., 1974.

Newman, Mildred and Berkowitz, Bernard. **How to Be Your Own Best Friend.** New York: Random House, 1971.

Olds, Sally Wendkos. "How to Handle a Compliment," **Today's Health,** February, 1975.

O'Neill, Nena and O'Neill, George. **Shifting Gears.** New York: Avon Books, 1975. Chapter 7, "Centering and Focusing."

Ornstein, A. C. "The Need For Research on Teaching the Disadvantaged," **Journal of Negro Education,** 40:133-138, 1971.

Patterson, C. H. "The Self in Recent Rogerian Theory," **Journal of Individual Psychology,** 1961, vol. 17, pp. 5-11.

Perls, Frederick S. **Ego, Hunger and Aggression.** New York: A Vintage Book, 1969.

——————. **Gestalt Therapy Verbatim.** Moab, Utah: Real People Press, 1969.

Polster, Erving and Miriam. **Gestalt Therapy Integrated.** New York: Vintage Books, Random House, 1974.

Powell, John, S. J. **The Secret of Staying in Love.** Niles, Illinois: Argus Communications Co., 1974.

——————. **Why Am I Afraid To Tell You Who I Am?** Niles, Illinois: Argus Communications Co., 1969.

——————. **Why Am I Afraid to Love?** Niles, Illinois: Argus Communications Co., 1972. Chapter 3, "The Self Image."

Purkey, William W. **Self Concept and School Achievement.** Englewood Cliffs, New Jersey: Prentice-Hall, Inc., 1970.

Rand, Ayn. **The Virtue of Selfishness: A New Concept of Egoism.** New York: Signet, 1964.

Randolph, Norma and Howe, William. **Self Enhancing Education.** Palo Alto, Ca.: Educational Progress Corp., 1966.

Rogers, Carl R. **Client-Centered Therapy.** Boston: Houghton Mifflin, 1951.

——————. "A Theory of Therapy, Personality, and Interpersonal Relationships, as Developed in the Client-Centered Framework," in Sigmund Koch, ed., **Psychology: A Study of a Science,** vol. 3. New York: McGraw-Hill, 1959, pp. 184-256.

_____. **On Becoming a Person.** Boston: Houghton Mifflin, 1961.

_____. "A Theory of Personality," in **Theories of Psychopathology and Personality,** ed., Theodore Millon. Phila.: W. B. Saunders, 1973, pp. 217-223.

Rosenberg, Morris. **Society and the Adolescent Self-Image.** Princeton, New Jersey: Princeton University Press, 1965.

Rotter, Julian B. and Hochreich, Dorothy J. **Personality.** Glenview, Illinois: Scott, Foresman & Co., 1975. Chapter 6, "Rogers' Self-Theory," pp. 67-79. Chapter 7, "Maslow's Holistic Theory," pp. 80-92.

Rubin, I. M. "Increased Self-Acceptance: A Means of Reducing Prejudice," **Journal of Personality and Social Psychology,** 5:223-38. 1967.

Rubin, Theodore I. **Dr. Rubin, Please Make Me Happy.** New York: Bantam Books, 1974. Chapter 1, "How Do You Feel About Yourself? Mind Image and Body Image," pp. 5-42.

Rucker, W. Ray, Arnspiger, V. Clyde and Brodbeck, Arthur J. **Human Values in Education.** Dubuque, Iowa: Kendall/Hunt Publishing Co., 1969. Chapter 6, "Enhancement of the Self-Image by Teachers and Students," pp. 118-137.

Satir, Virginia. "Conjoint Marital Therapy" in **The Psychotherapies of Marital Disharmony,** ed., Bernard L. Green, pp. 121-134. New York: The Free Press, 1965.

_____. **Conjoint Family Therapy,** revised ed. Palo Alto, Ca.: Science and Behavior Books, 1967. Chapter II, "Low Self-Esteem and Mate Selection." Chapter VI, "What All Children Need in Order to Have Self-Esteem."

_____. **Peoplemaking.** Palo Alto, Ca.: Science and Behavior Books, Inc., 1972.

Schmuck, Richard A. and Patricia A. Schmuck. **A Humanistic Psychology of Education**—Making the School Everybody's House. Palo Alto, Ca.: National Press Books, 1974.

Schuller, Robert H. **Self-Love**—The Dynamic Force of Success. New York: Hawthorn Books, Inc., 1969.

Schutz, William C. **Here Comes Everybody**—Everyman's Guide to Encounter. New York: Harper and Row, Harrow Books, 1972. "The Self-Concept," pp. 13-21.

Seabury, David. **The Art of Selfishness.** New York: Pocket Books, 1974.

Sear, Pauline, S. and Vivian S. Sherman. **In Pursuit of Self-Esteem.** Belmont, Ca.: Wadsworth Publishing Co., 1964.

Severin, Frank T., ed. **Humanistic Viewpoints in Psychology.** New York: McGraw-Hill Book Co., 1965.

Snygg, D. and Arthur D. Combs. **Individual Behavior.** New York: Harper and Row, 1949.

Stein, Joseph. **Effective Personality: A Humanistic Approach.** Belmont, Ca.: Brooks/Cole Publishing Co., 1972.

Steiner, Claude. **Games Alcoholics Play.** New York: Grove Press, Inc., 1971.

_____. **Scripts People Live:** Transactional Analysis of Life Scripts. New York: Grove Press, Inc., 1974.

_____, et al. **Readings in Radical Psychiatry.** Chapter 3, "The Stroke Economy," by Claude Steiner. Chapter 4, "Women's Scripts and the Stroke Economy," by Hogie Wyckoff.

Strang, Ruth. **Helping Your Child Develop His Potentialities.** New York: Award Books, 1970.

Stringer, Lorene A. **The Sense of Self**—A Guide to How We Mature. Phila.: Temple University Press, 1971. Chapter 3, "About Mirrors, Images, and the Self," pp. 46-82.

Sullivan, Harry Stack. **The Interpersonal Theory of Psychiatry.** New York: W. W. Norton, 1953.

Tegeler, Bill and Carole. **The People Press—Life-Script Awareness.** La Jolla, Ca.: University Associates, 1975.

Thompson, Warren. **Correlates of the Self Concept.** Nashville, Tenn.: Counselor Recordings and Tests, 1972.

Tillich, Paul. **The Courage to Be.** New Haven: Yale University Press, 1959.

Tobin, Stephen A. "Wholeness and Self-Support," **Gestalt Is,** ed. John O. Stevens, pp. 121-147. Moab, Utah: Real People Press, 1975.

Valette, Robert. **Self-Actualization**—A Guide to Happiness and Self-Determination. Niles, Ill.: Argus Communications, 1974. Chapter 16, "Self-Confidence and Celebration," pp. 91-5.

Wagner, Maurice E. **Put It All Together**—Developing Inner Security. Grand Rapids, Mich.: Zondervan Publishing House, 1974.

_____. **The Sensation of Being Somebody**—Building an Adequate Self-Concept. Grand Rapids, Mich.: Zondervan Publishing House, 1975.

Webster, Murray and Barbara Sobieszek. **Sources of Self-Evaluation:** A Formal Theory of Significant Others and Social Influence. New York: John Wiley & Sons, Inc., 1974.

Wells, L. Edward and Gerald Marwell. **Self-Esteem: Its Conceptualization and Measurement.** Beverly Hills, Ca.: Sage Publications, 1975.

Wells, Theodora. "Women's Self-Concept: Implications for Managerial Development," in **Optimizing Human Resources,** Gordon L. Lippitt, et al, eds. Reading, Mass.: Addison-Wesley Publishing Co., 1971. pp. 302-312.

Williams, Roger J. **You Are Extraordinary.** New York: Pyramid Books, 1974.

Wylie, Ruth C. **The Self Concept.** Lincoln, Neb.: The University of Nebraska Press, 1961.

Yamamoto, Kaoru, ed. **The Child and His Image**—Self Concept in the Early Years. Boston: Houghton Mifflin Co., 1972.

B. GROUP EXERCISES, ACTIVITIES AND PROGRAMS
FOR HUMAN RELATIONS TRAINING

Bach, George (with Yetta Bernhard). **Aggression Lab**—The Fair Fight Training Manual. Dubuque, Iowa: Kendall/Hunt Publishing Co., 1971.

Bolton, Robert. **Values Clarification for Educators.** Cazenovia, New York: Ridge Consultants, 1975.

_____. **A Workbook in Values Clarification.** Cazenovia, New York: Ridge Consultants, 1975.

Brayer, Herbert O. and Zella W. Cleary. **Valuing in the Family**—A Workshop Guide for Parents. San Diego, Ca.: Pennant Press, 1972.

Canfield, Jack and Harold C. Wells. **100 Ways to Enhance Self-Concept in the Classroom**—a Handbook for Teachers and Parents. Englewood Cliffs, New Jersey: Prentice-Hall, 1976.

Caplan, Gerald. **Principles of Preventive Psychiatry.** New York: Basic Books, 1964.

Carkhuff, Robert R. **Helping and Human Relations.** Vols. I and II. New York: Holt, Rinehart and Winston, 1969.

_____. **The Development of Human Resources.** New York: Holt, Rinehart and Winston, 1971.

_____. **The Art of Helping—An Introduction to Life Skills (Trainer's Guide).** Amherst, Mass.: Human Resource Development Press, Inc., 1975.

Crampton, Martha. "The Use of Mental Imagery in Psychosynthesis," **Journal of Humanistic Psychology,** Fall, 1969.

Desoille, Robert. **The Directed Daydream.** New York: Psychosynthesis Research Foundation, Inc., 1966.

Egan, Gerard. **Encounter: Group Processes for Interpersonal Growth.** Belmont, Ca.: Brooks/Cole Publishing Co., 1970.

_____.**Face to Face**—The Small-Group Experience and Interpersonal Growth. Belmont, Ca.: Brooks/Cole Publishing Co., 1973.

Flynn, Elizabeth W. and John F. LaFaso. **Designs in Affective Education.** New York: Paulist Press, 1974.

Gazda, George M. **Human Relations Development**—a Manual for Educators. Boston: Allyn and Bacon, 1973.

Geyer, Nancy and Shirley Noll. **Team Building in Church Groups.** Valley Forge, Pa.: Judson Press, 1970.

Golembiewski, Robert T. and Arthur Blumberg, eds. **Sensitivity Training and the Laboratory Approach.** 2nd ed. Itasca, Ill.: F.E. Peacock Publishers, Inc., 1973.

Hawley, Robert C. and Isabel L. Hawley. **A Handbook of Personal Growth Activities for Classroom Use.** Amherst, Mass.: Education Research Associates Press, 1972.

_____. **Developing Human Potential: A Handbook of Activities for Personal and Social Growth.** Amherst, Mass.: Education Research Associates Press, 1975.

Henderson, C. William. **Awakening:** Ways to Psychospiritual Growth. Englewood Cliffs, New Jersey: Prentice-Hall, 1975. Chapter 1, "Meeting Your Subconscious."

Hendrix, John and Lela. **Experiential Education: X-Ed.** Nashville, Tenn.: Abingdon, 1975.

Howe, Leland W. and Mary M. Howe. **Personalizing Education**—Values Clarification and Beyond. New York: Hart Publishing Co., 1975. Part I, chapter 5, "Building Students' Self-Concepts," pp. 81-108.

Jongeward, Dorothy and Muriel James. **Winning With People**—Group Exercises in Transactional Analysis. Reading, Mass.: Addison-Wesley Publishing Co., 1973.

King, Ruth G. **"'I Am Somebody'**—Black Students' Self-Concept." **Social Change: Ideas and Applications,** vol. 4, No. 1, 1974. Arlington, Va.: NTL Institute for Applied Behavioral Science.

Lakin, Martin. "Group Sensitivity Training and Encounter: Uses and Abuses of a Method." **The Counseling Psychologist,** 1970, vol. 2 (#2), pp. 66-70.

Lewis, Howard R. and Harold S. Streitfeld. **Growth Games.** New York: Bantam Books, 1972.

Lippitt, Gordon L., Leslie E. This and Leslie E. Bidwell, Jr., eds. **Optimizing Human Resources.** Reading, Mass.: Addison-Wesley Publishing Co., 1971. Chapter 5, "Laboratory Training in Developing Human Potential," pp. 213-247.

Luft, Joseph. **Group Processes**—An Introduction to Group Dynamics, 2nd. ed. Palo Alto, Ca.: National Press Books, 1970.

——————. **Of Human Interaction.** Palo Alto, Ca.: Mayfield Publishing Co., 1969.

Malamud, Daniel I. and Solomon Machover. **Toward Self-Understanding**—Group Techniques in Self-Confrontation. Springfield, Ill.: Charles C. Thomas Publisher, 1970.

Morrison, Eleanor S. and Mila Underhill Price. **Values in Sexuality**—A New Approach to Sex Education. New York: Hart Publishing Co., 1974.

Moustakas, Clark. **The Authentic Teacher**—Sensitivity and Awareness in the Classroom. Cambridge, Mass.: Howard A. Doyle Publishing Co., 1966.

Mylen, Donald, et al. **Handbook of Staff Development and Human Relations Training.** Washington, D.C.: NTL Institute for Applied Behavioral Sciences, 1967.

Napier, Rodney W. and Matti K. Gershenfeld. **Instructor's Manual—Group's: Theory and Experience.** Boston: Houghton Mifflin Co., 1973.

——————. **Groups: Theory and Experience.** Boston: Houghton Mifflin Co., 1973.

Otto, Herbert A. **Groups Methods to Actualize Human Potential:** A Handbook. Beverly Hills, Ca.: The Holistic Press, 1973.

——————. **A Guide to Developing Your Potential.** No. Hollywood, Ca.: Wilshire Publishing Co., 1974.

Our Bodies, Our Selves: A Course by and for Women. The Boston Health

Collective, Simon and Schuster, 1973.

Palomares, Uvaldo Hill and Geraldine Ball. **Magic Circle—An Overview of the Human Development Program.** La Mesa, Ca.: Human Development Training Institute, 1974.

Peterson, Audrey J. **Motivation Advance Program.** Rosemont, Ill.: Combined Motivation Education Systems, 6300 River Road, 60018.

Pfeiffer, J. William and John E. Jones. **A Handbook of Structured Experiences for Human Relations Training,** vols. I-VI. La Jolla, Ca.: University Associates, 1970-1978.

_____eds. **The Annual Handbook for Group Facilitators,** vol. I—1972; vol. II—1973; vol. III—1974; vol. IV—1975. La Jolla, Ca.: University Associates, 1972, 1973, 1974, 1975, 1976, 1977, 1978.

Raths, Louis E., Merrill Harmin and Sidney B. Simon. **Values and Teaching.** Columbus, Ohio: Charles E. Merrill Publishing Co., 1966.

Reichert, Richard. **Self-Awareness Through Group Dynamics.** Dayton, Ohio: Pflaum Publishing, 1970.

Rucker, W. Ray, V. Clyde Arnspiger, Arthur J. Brodbeck. **Human Values in Education.** Dubuque, Iowa: Kendall/Hunt Publishing Co., 1969.

Saulnier, Leda and Teresa Simard. **Personal Growth and Interpersonal Relations.** Englewood Cliffs, New Jersey: Prentice-Hall, 1973. Chapter 15, "Success and Your Self-Image," pp. 171-179.

Savary, Louis M. **Integrating Values.** Theory and Exercises for Clarifying and Integrating Religious Values. Dayton, Ohio: Pflaum Publishing, 1974.

Sax, Saville and Sandra Hollander. **Reality Games.** New York: The Macmillan Co., 1972.

Schrank, Jeffrey. **Teaching Human Beings**—101 Subversive Activities for the Classroom. Boston: Beacon Press, 1972.

Seldman, Martin and David Hermes. **Personal Growth Through Groups.** San Diego: We Care Foundation, 1975.

Shorr, Joseph E. **Psycho-Imagination Therapy.** The Integration of Phenomenology and Imagination. New York: Intercontinental Medical Book Corp., 1972.

Simon, Sidney B. **Meeting Yourself Halfway.** 31 Value Clarification Strategies for Daily Living. Niles, Ill.: Argus Communications, 1974. Strategy 13, "A Matter of Pride"—Things I am proud of...., pp. 54-58.

_____. **Caring, Feeling, Touching.** Niles, Ill.: Argus Communications, 1976.

_____. **Vulture.** Niles, Ill.: Argus Communications, 1977.

_____. **I Am Loveable and Capable.** A Modern Allegory on the Classical Put-Down. Niles, Ill.: Argus Communications, 1973.

_____, Leland W. Howe and Howard Kirschenbaum. **Values Clarification**—A Handbook of Practical Strategies. New York: Hart Publishing Co., 1972.

_____ and Jay Clark. **More Values Clarification**—Strategies for the Classroom. San Diego, Ca.: Pennant Press, 1975.

_____ and Howard Kirschenbaum, eds. **Readings in Values**

Clarification. Minneapolis, Minn.: Winston Press, Inc., 1973.

_____. "Please Touch!—How to Combat Skin Hunger in Our Schools." **Scholastic Teacher,** October, 1974, pp. 22-25.

Simpson, Bert K. **Becoming Aware of Values.** San Diego, Ca.: Pennant Press, 1973.

Siroka, Robert W., Ellen K. Siroka and Gilbert A. Schloss. **Sensitivity Training and Group Encounter.** New York: Grosset and Dunlap, 1971.

Smalheiser, Lawrence. **Self Encounter.** Los Angeles, Ca.: Price/Stern/Sloan, 1973.

Timmerman, Tim and Jim Ballard. **Strategies in Humanistic Education,** Vol. I. Amherst, Mass.: Mandala, 1975. "Self-Concept," pp. 61-71.

Valett, Robert. **Self-Actualization.** Niles, Ill.: Argus Communications, 1974. Chapter 16, "Self-Confidence and Celebration," pp. 91-94.

Weinstein, Gerald and Mario D. Fantini. **Toward Humanistic Education— A Curriculum of Affect.** New York: Praeger, 1970. Pp. 91-93, Lesson 7, "Strong-Point Glasses."

Wells, Harold C. and John T. Canfield. **About Me**—Student Book. **About Me**—Teachers Guide. Chicago, Ill.: Encyclopedia Britannica Educational Corp., 1971.

Wood, John. **How Do You Feel?** A Guide to Your Emotions. Englewood Cliffs, New Jersey: Prentice-Hall, 1974.

C. MINORITY GROUPS AND THEIR SELF-CONCEPT

Anderson, James M. "Developing Criteria for Evaluating Ethnic Studies Materials," **Audiovisual Instruction,** November, 1972.

Banks, James A. and Jean D. Grambs. **Black Self-Concept**—Implications for Education and Social Science. New York: McGraw-Hill Book Co., 1972.

Barnes, Edward J. "The Black Community as the Source of Positive Self-Concept for Black Children: A Theoretical Perspective," **Black Psychology,** ed., Reginald L. Jones. New York: Harper and Row, 1972, pp. 166-192.

Becker, William H. "Black and Jew: Ambivalence and Affinities," **Soundings,** Volume 53, 1970, pp. 413-439.

Bernstein, Peretz. **Jew-Hate as a Sociological Problem.** New York: Philosophical Society, 1951. "Jewish Anti-Semitism," pp. 280-6.

Borowitz, Eugene. **The Masks Jews Wear:** Self-Deceptions of American Jewry. New York: Simon and Schuster, 1973.

Broderick, Francis L. and August Meier. **Negro Protest Thought in the Twentieth Century.** New York: Bobbs-Merrill, 1965. "The Negro Artist and the Racial Mountain" by Langston Hughes, pp. 92-97.

Carter, Thomas P. "The Negative Self-Concept of Mexican-American Students," **School and Society,** 96:217-219. March 30, 1968.

Chapman, Abraham, ed. **New Black Voices.** An Anthology of Contemporary Afro-American Literature. New York: The New American

Library, 1972 (A Mentor Book). "Black Power," p. 316, "Excellence of Soul," pp. 583-5.

Cheek, Donald K. **Assertive Black/Puzzled White.** San Luis Obispo, Ca.: Impact Publishers, 1978.

Clark, Kenneth B. **Dark Ghetto.** New York: Harper and Row, 1965.

Cottle, T.J. **Black Children, White Dreams.** Boston: Houghton Mifflin, 1974.

Cross, Jr., William. "The Negro-to-Black Conversion Experience," **Black World,** Vol. 20, #9, July, 1971, pp. 13-27.

Deloria, Jr., Vine. **We Talk, You Listen**—New Tribes, New Turf. New York: Macmillan, 1970. Chapter 2, "Stereotyping," pp. 33-44.

Elkins, Dov Peretz. "Jews and Blacks—Past, Present, Future," **The Reconstructionist,** May 17, 1968.

_____. **Loving My Jewishness: Jewish Self-Esteem and Self-Pride.** Rochester, N.Y.: Growth Associates, 1978.

Frerichs, Allen H. "Relationship of Self-Esteem of the Disadvantaged to School Success," **Journal of Negro Education,** 40:117-120, 1971.

Glustrom, Simon. **The Language of Judaism,** 2nd ed. New York: Ktav Publishing Co., 1972. "Mah Yafit—Subservient Jew," pp. 96-7.

Greenberg, Sidney, ed. **A Modern Treasury of Jewish Thoughts.** New York: Yoseloff, 1960. Chapter 1, "To Be or Not to Be a Jew," pp. 23-50.

Greer, Colin, ed. **Divided Society: The Ethnic Experience in America.** New York: Basic Books, 1974.

Grier, W.H. and Price M. Cobbs. **Black Rage.** New York: Basic Books, 1968.

Hayakawa, S.I. **Symbol, Status, and Personality.** New York: Harcourt, Brace and World, 1963. Chapter 6, "The Self-Image and Intercultural Understanding, or How to Be Sane Though Negro," pp. 70-88.

Herman, Judith, ed. **The Schools and Group Identity.** New York: American Jewish Committee, 1974 (Institute on Pluralism and Group Identity).

Howard, John R., ed. **Awakening Minorities**—American Indians, Mexican Americans, Puerto Ricans. New Brunswick, New Jersey: Aldine Publishing Co., 1970.

Josephy, Jr., Alvin M. **Red Power**—The American Indian's Fight for Freedom. New York: McGraw Hill Book Co., 1972.

Kahane, Meir. **Never Again.** Los Angeles, Ca.: Nash Publishing Co., 1971. "Jewish Pride," pp. 133-164.

King, Ruth G. "'I Am Somebody'—Black Students' Self-Concept," H.L. Fromkin and J.J. Sherwood, eds., **Intergroup and Minority Relations,** pp. 22-28. La Jolla, Ca.: University Associates, 1976.

Lewin, Kurt. **Resolving Social Conflicts.** New York: Harper & Bros., 1948. Chapter 11, "Bringing Up the Jewish Child," pp. 169-185; chapter 12, "Self-Hatred Among Jews," pp. 186-220.

Lieberman, Chaim. **The Grave Concern.** New York: Shengold, 1968. Chapter 22, "Education for Self-Hatred," pp. 131-138.

Lincoln, C. Eric. **The Black Muslims in America** (Rev. ed.) Boston: Beacon Press, 1973. Chapter 2, "The Dynamics of Black Nationalism," pp. 35-51.

Littleton, Arthur C. and Mary W. Burger. **Black View-Points.** New York: New American Library, a Mentor Book, 1971.

Maliver, Bruce L. "Anti-Negro Bias Among Negro College Students," **Journal of Personality and Social Psychology,** 1965, Vol. 2, pp. 770-775.

Perlmutter, Philip. "Ethnic Education: Can it be relevant?" **The Massachusetts Teacher,** February, 1974.

Petuchowski, Jakob J. "Prophetic Religion, Jewish Self-Interest and the American Scene." New York: The Jewish Rights Council, 1972.

Phelps, Stanlee and Nancy Austin. **The Assertive Woman.** San Luis Obispo, Ca.: Impact Publishers, 1977.

Riesman, David. "A Philosophy for 'Minority' Living," The Jewish Situation and the 'Nerve of Failure,' **Commentary,** Vol. 6, #5, 1948.

Rubin, I.M. "Increased Self-Acceptance: A Means of Reducing Prejudice," **Journal of Personality and Social Psychology,** 5:233-238, 1967.

Sarnoff, I. "Identification with the aggressor: Some personality correlates of anti-Semitism among Jews." **Journal of Personality,** 1951, Vol. 20, pp. 199-218.

_____. **Identification With the Aggressor: Some Personality Correlates of Anti-Semitism Among Jews.** Unpublished doctoral dissertation, University of Michigan, 1951.

Sartre, Jean-Paul. **Anti-Semite and Jew.** New York: Schocken, 1948. "The Inauthentic Jew," pp. 94-141.

Segalman, R. **A Test of the Lewinian Hypothesis on Self-Hatred Among the Jews.** Unpublished doctoral thesis, New York University, 1967.

Shapiro, Manheim S. "Changing Jewish Attitudes—And Their Consequences for Jewish Community Relations Workers," **Journal of Jewish Communal Service,** Vol. 37, Summer, 1961, pp. 405-410.

Sherman, C. Bezalel. **The Jew Within American Society.** Detroit: Wayne State University Press, 1965. Chapter 12, "The Self-Image of the American Jew," pp. 217-227.

Singer, Howard. **Bring Forth the Mighty Men.** New York: Funk and Wagnalls, 1969. About Cousin Merwyn, pp. 230-233.

Steinberg, Milton. **A Partisan Guide to the Jewish Problem.** New York: Bobbs-Merrill Co., 1945. Chapter 7, "The Sick Soul," pp. 115-129.

Wilmore, Jr., Gayraud S. "Ethnic Identities and Christian Theology," **Nexus,** Winter, 1972-3, Vol. XVI, #1.

Wright, Jr., Nathan. **Let's Work Together.** New York: Hawthorn Books, Inc., 1968. Chapter 6. "Knowing the Beauty of What We Are," pp. 117-143.

Wyckoff, Hogie. "Women's Scripts and the Stroke Economy," in Claude Steiner, ed., **Readings in Radical Psychiatry.** New York: Grove Press, 1975, pp. 44-54.

157

EXPERIENTIAL LEARNING
Finally, A New, Exciting And Enjoyable Way To Learn

Dr. Dov Peretz Elkins is a pioneer in the field of psychology, education and human development. He combines the wisdom, experience, training and insight of the talmudic sage and the modern behavioral scientist.

He has produced a series of important and valuable volumes on a new, exciting, challenging, and growth-producing way to learn. To learn about yourself, about how to establish meaningful relationships, how to strengthen family life, and about the art/science of becoming a self-actualizing, fully-mature, fully functioning human being.

Send order form below to: Growth Associates, Human Relations Consultants and Publishers, Box 18429, Rochester, NY 14618-0429, 716/244-1225.

QUANTITY	TITLES BY DR. ELKINS	PRICE
	Twelve Pathways to Feeling Better About Yourself. An inspirational book for general and professional reader. $7.50	
	Self-Concept Sourcebook: Ideas and Activities for Building Self-Esteem. A collection of extended writings of leading psychologists and educators, including Rogers, Fromm, Canfield, Hamachek, Horney, Purkey, plus many new learning exercises and activities. $16.	
	Humanizing Jewish Life: Judaism & the Human Potential Movement $12.50	
	Teaching People to Love Themselves: A Leader's Handbook of Theory & Technique for Self-Esteem Training $19.50.	
	Glad To Be Me: Building Self-Esteem in Yourself & Others $9.50.	
	Cassette Tapes ($10 each) a) Be Glad to Be You—the Magic of Self-Esteem b) Relaxation and Self-Esteem Building Exercise c) Enhancing Self-Concept in the Classroom d) New Frontiers in Spiritual Development e) Growing the Life of the Spirit	

Name _____

Address _____

City _____ State _____ Zip _____

All orders **must** be prepaid. Prices include postage & handling.

☐ Check here if interested in information on lectures, workshops and/or other training events.

Subtotal _____
NY residents add 7% tax
Total Order _____
Canadians use U.S. funds or add 15% _____
TOTAL ORDER _____

EXPERIENTIAL LEARNING
Finally, A New, Exciting And Enjoyable Way To Learn

Dr. Dov Peretz Elkins is a pioneer in the field of psychology, education and human development. He combines the wisdom, experience, training and insight of the talmudic sage and the modern behavioral scientist.

He has produced a series of important and valuable volumes on a new, exciting, challenging, and growth-producing way to learn. To learn about yourself, about how to establish meaningful relationships, how to strengthen family life, and about the art/science of becoming a self-actualizing, fully-mature, fully functioning human being.

Send order form below to: Growth Associates, Human Relations Consultants and Publishers, Box 18429, Rochester, NY 14618-0429, 716/244-1225.

QUANTITY	TITLES BY DR. ELKINS	PRICE
	Twelve Pathways to Feeling Better About Yourself. An inspirational book for general and professional reader. $7.50	
	Self-Concept Sourcebook: Ideas and Activities for Building Self-Esteem. A collection of extended writings of leading psychologists and educators, including Rogers, Fromm, Canfield, Hamachek, Horney, Purkey, plus many new learning exercises and activities. $16.	
	Humanizing Jewish Life: Judaism & the Human Potential Movement $12.50	
	Teaching People to Love Themselves: A Leader's Handbook of Theory & Technique for Self-Esteem Training $19.50.	
	Glad To Be Me: Building Self-Esteem in Yourself & Others $9.50.	
	Cassette Tapes ($10 each) a) Be Glad to Be You—the Magic of Self-Esteem b) Relaxation and Self-Esteem Building Exercise c) Enhancing Self-Concept in the Classroom d) New Frontiers in Spiritual Development e) Growing the Life of the Spirit	

Name _____

Address _____

City _____ State _____ Zip _____

All orders **must** be prepaid. Prices include postage & handling.

☐ Check here if interested in information on lectures, workshops and/or other training events.

Subtotal _____

NY residents add 7% tax

Total Order _____

Canadians use U.S. funds or add 15% _____

TOTAL ORDER _____